"Watch Out for the Foreign Guests!"

The China Reader
Modern China
The Town That Fought To Save Itself
In The People's Republic
Brown

"Watch Out for the Foreign Guests!"

China Encounters the West

Orville Schell

Pantheon Books
New York

LIBRARY OF CONGRESS CATALOGING IN PUBLICATION DATA

Schell, Orville.
"Watch out for the foreign guests!"

1. China—Civilization—1949—
—Occidental influences.   I.   Title.
DS724.S3   951.05   80–7714
ISBN 0–394–51331–2

Manufactured in the United States of America
FIRST EDITION

Grateful acknowledgment is made to the following for permission to reprint previously published material:

Willie Nelson Music Company: Portion of lyrics from "Whiskey River" by Johnny Bush Shinn.

United Artists Music: Portion of lyrics from "The Wild Side of Life" by William Warren and Arlie Carter. Copyright © 1952 by Unart Music Corporation.

For Meredith

ACKNOWLEDGMENTS

The help that I received in preparing this book was bountiful. I want to thank Deborah Perrin for her stenographic help, and Burr Heneman, Joseph Esherick, and John Service for reading various stages of the manuscript and not being timid in their criticism. For Tom Engelhardt, my friend and editor at Pantheon, and one of the few perfectionist editors in publishing who works as hard on his books as do his authors, my deep thanks. And for Meredith Tromble, to whom this book is dedicated and who has edited each of these pages so many times that she doubtless knows most by heart, thanks are hardly enough.

—Orville Schell
May 1980

"Watch Out for the Foreign Guests!"

When Bob Hope appeared on American TV in the fall of 1979 hoofing his way down the Great Wall wearing two-tone shoes, a blue Mao cap, a sports shirt, and swinging his famed golf club, it was obvious that an era had drawn to a close in China. As he crooned before the NBC cameras, "We're on the road to China! Who knows what we're gonna find?" while "chop-chop" music right out of a Fu Manchu movie accompanied, the Thoughts of Chairman Mao seemed far away indeed.

The specter of Bob Hope, court jester to the U.S. military, shuffling insouciantly across an ancient Chinese landmark was one that took some getting used to. What supercharged the moment was not so much what Hope wore or sang but the fact that he was there at all. Hope's routine seemed like a ritual victory dance celebrating the triumph of the American way of life over China's Maoist revolution, which had for so many years resisted just such Western depredation.

"The Great Wall of China!" quipped Hope as he continued his almost taunting parody. "It's an unbelievable sight! It's the greatest job of construction this side of Raquel Welch!"

A moment later, appearing before the majestic Gate of Heavenly Peace through which emperors used to enter the Imperial City, and on top of which Mao used to stand to review his followers parading past, Hope launched into a series of one-liners. He cracked jokes about the laundry service at the Peking Hotel and how the Forbidden City, the old imperial residence, looked "just like Las Vegas without the slot machines."

Standing alone in the vastness of Tiananmen Square as workers, bicycling past, craned their necks in wonderment, Hope belted out his gags.

"Take a look at it!" Hope told his American viewers, gesturing across the square toward the Great Hall of the People.

"It looks just like Jackie Gleason's patio." He might as well have been standing in front of St. Peter's Basilica in the Vatican comparing it to the Houston Astrodome.

"Hey! This is it! Peking, China!" he continued, accompanied by a laugh track in no way related to the quizzical comrades gliding by him.

"Amazing, isn't it? Just ten years ago, who would have dreamt that an American comedian would be standing here in Tiananmen Square, saying whatever he pleased?"

Who indeed?

As I sat in front of my television set in California, the appearance of the once-forbidden landmarks of Peking punctuated by Bob Hope as well as Coca-Cola, Texaco, and Du Pont commercials made it seem as if the very foundations of China had shifted. Only a few years ago, the idea of Bob Hope filming a show-biz spectacular in the People's Republic of China would have been inconceivable. In fact, it was exactly the tenacity with which China's Marxist leaders had long warded off such foreign incursions that now made Hope's NBC special so jarring.

Far from being politically meaningless entertainment, Hope's presence in Peking, and later in Shanghai, suggested the degree to which China had decided to relax its vigilant defense of its country and people against cultural and political contamination from the bourgeois world outside.

Although the NBC program notes for the TV special boasted that "Hope helped China and the U.S. take a giant step toward bringing the two countries still closer together culturally," "Ole Ski Nose's" performance in China was more of a collision than a cultural exchange. Had the Chinese wished to engineer a starker confrontation between the values of the West and those which they had so strenuously espoused over the last thirty years, it would be hard to think just how they might have done so more successfully.

That part of me which had secretly admired Chinese resistance to the homogenizing effects of Western culture felt almost betrayed by the Chinese invitation to Hope to come and use their country like a Hollywood soundstage. True, Richard Nixon, Henry Kissinger, and Gerald Ford had all written letters to the Chinese government on behalf of their cultural patron saint, but, in the end, it was the Chinese themselves who had agreed to let Hope in. What happened to China's protectionist instinct, which had seemed almost historically encoded in its genes since the first Westerners arrived off the South China coast in the early sixteenth century? What did China's leaders have in mind when they turned the Temple of Heaven (built by the Yonglo emperor in 1420 to perform cosmic sacrifices) over to Peaches and Herb, another part of Hope's show, as a backdrop for their pop disco hit "We've Got Love"?

Where was it leading?

It had not always been as easy for foreigners to breach China as it was for Bob Hope. In the past, the Chinese had been renowned for their arrogant sense of self-sufficiency and cultural superiority, so strong that when Westerners did finally arrive, China's first instinct was to shut them out.

"We possess all things," the Qianlong emperor had complacently written to King George III in 1793 on the arrival of an English ambassador in Peking in search of free trade and diplomatic relations. "I set no value on things strange and ingenious and have no use for your country's manufacturers," he added haughtily. Qianlong simply wanted these "foreign barbarians," as the Chinese then called all Westerners, to disappear without taking offense and leave China alone.

But, of course, the Westerners did not simply vanish. With little sensitivity to China's distaste for their strange ways, the Westerners began using their superior military technology to batter their way in. That the Chinese did not welcome them

—in fact, viewed them as inferiors from beyond the margins of the civilized world (*their* world)—did not deter these European interlopers in the slightest.

In fact, from the early sixteenth century when the first Portuguese traders appeared off the South China coast until recently, the history of China's relations with the West were fraught with trouble. A technologically inferior China struggled futilely to stem the tide of foreign incursion. Weakness and disunity doomed China to be "sliced like a melon" by the stronger Western powers.

In 1949, thirty-eight years after the fall of the last imperial dynasty, Mao's Communist government came to power. Following a brief attempt to come to terms with America in the 1940s (efforts which the U.S. rebuffed), China and the U.S. became engaged on opposite sides: first, in the Chinese Civil War; and then the Korean War. During this period, Mao tried "leaning" to the other side and signed a friendship pact with the Soviet Union. When that failed disastrously in the late 1950s, Mao seemed determined to adopt a more traditionally Chinese posture toward the Western world. Old antipathies against "foreign barbarians" merged with ideological aversions to imperialists, capitalists, and revisionists, creating a new and unyielding attitude toward foreign intrusion of any variety.

Calling for "self-reliance" and "vigilance" against the foes of China and its socialist revolution, Mao ushered in an era of relative isolation suggestive of the dynastic period. For most Americans, China again seemed as distant and unknowable as it had during the reign of the Qianlong emperor.

It was this sense of isolation, the Chinese leadership's reluctance to willingly expose the Chinese people to the outside world and its ideas, which first attracted me to China.

Like a renowned personage who refuses all interviews and turns away all visitors, China in its inaccessibility was magnetic. Of course, her long history and rich culture held a fascination of their own. But for a young college student in the late 1950s, these features were eclipsed by one simple and compelling fact: as an American student, one could not go to China. Although it was true that a few Americans, "friends of China," were granted visas (only to have their passports seized by the American government on return), normal avenues of access and exchange were closed. Shrouded in a veil of impenetrability, the People's Republic of China became an alluring Communist mystery.

As I studied in the windowless basement stacks of the Harvard-Yenching Institute, surrounded by tens of thousands of Chinese books, China seemed a little less remote. Like moonrocks, those silent volumes provided a concrete connection with their distant homeland. Sitting in their midst was at once reassuring and provoking. Like many other budding Sinologists, I would often find myself thinking up ways to penetrate what was then called "the bamboo curtain" between the U.S. and China. But letters to Peking went unanswered. Contacts with European diplomats who had been to China came to nought. Trips to Chinese embassies in Third World countries produced nothing more than brief encounters with opaque officials.

China was frustrating, but it also aroused the explorer's instinct, a most un-Chinese impulse, in those of us who were in pursuit. Whereas the Chinese had historically shown little interest in seafaring explorations to the world beyond their shores, we Westerners had long sought to break down such barriers to penetrate the heart of hostile geographic environments, reclusive civilizations, or even outer space. As in the past, China's closure seemed once again to call forth this conquering instinct.

Trips around China's periphery in the 1960s offered little satisfaction. Hong Kong, that minuscule enclave of Western commerce clinging to the Chinese coast, was little more than an infuriating tease. It was so close that, from the New Territories, one could actually gaze out over the water and see the hills of China. But, though two Hong Kong–Canton Railroad Line tracks crossed the Lowu Bridge into China at Shenzhen, visa-less Americans knew these were not meant for them.

While riding the Star Ferry from Kowloon to the Victoria side, I would jealously watch the junks flying Communist Chinese flags as they sailed the Pearl River between Hong Kong and Canton.

I think that American China-watchers would have felt less checkmated if there had been no possibility of access at all. Instead, we had to learn to live with our specific lack of access, tantalized by unrealizable possibilities.

I remember lying awake in the wet winter rawness and the suffocating summer heat of Taibei, capital of Chiang Kai-shek's China, the one we were still welcome in, dreaming of the real China. Sometimes when the heat and humidity were unbearable, student friends and I would ride a bus out to the north coast of Taiwan. Getting off at a certain fishing village, we would stretch out on the white, deserted beach and surreptitiously tune in Radio Peking on a battery-powered transistor set. The "Chinese Mainland" was in front of us, only a hundred miles away across the Taiwan Strait. We felt thrilled indeed, listening to the illegal broadcasts of the "Communist bandits," as Chiang's government called them.

The refusal of Mao to welcome Americans to China was, of course, only one element in our exclusion. The other was the American government, whose implacable opposition to the Chinese Communists was every bit as passionate as China's anti-American disposition. This mutual distaste seemed to fuel itself into ascending spirals of antipathy, so that when Secretary of State John Foster Dulles met Zhou Enlai in Geneva in 1954, Dulles icily walked past him, refusing even a perfunctory handshake. Each of these historic moments made the hope of reconciliation only more remote, underscoring the chasm between our two worlds. But ironically, the more inconceivable the thought of going to China was, the more compelling it became.

In addition to the impossibility of actually traveling to the mainland, there was something else which drew me to China. From a distance China seemed to defy the forces which ruled the rest of the world. "Communist China" appeared to operate according to an entirely different set of political laws. The Chinese seemed to take pride in their professed inviolability to the economic and political dictums of the world outside. They had no Hilton Hotels, no branches of the Chase Manhattan Bank. They accepted no American Express cards, imported no Hollywood movies, sold no Western consumer goods, seemed oblivious to Western fashions, and courted no foreign aid. In fact, they boasted of their freedom from the world market system and scorned those nations which had capitulated to foreign loans or become reliant on foreign technical advice and enamored of foreign culture. China, the former "sick man of Asia," cultivated the image of being suspended above the imperatives that ruled other nations.

It was this apparent ability to survive and develop without props from the Great Powers that made China all the more astonishing. Its stubborn refusal to subordinate itself to any of the capitalist or imperialist powers which surrounded it lent China an aura of purity and defiance.

In the absence of concrete reality, it was all too easy to fantasize about China. But it was unclear whether these images of self-direction and resourcefulness sprang from the reforming powers of Maoist thought, whether they were reincarnations of China's age-old tendency to view itself as superior and self-sufficient, or whether they were just the creations of propaganda. Whatever their source, in a world where other developing nations were mired in problems clearly beyond their control, China seemed a hopeful land apart.

By the time I finally made it into China in 1975, to work first on a model farm and then in a Shanghai factory, more than a decade had elapsed since the experience on the beach in Taiwan. Mao still lived, and China still jealously guarded her independence and separation from the rest of the world. Although a trickle of Americans were beginning to visit, one still had the sensation at the border of entering an entirely new universe. What made the moment of crossing so extraordinary was not only that a visa put one among the chosen few, but that once over the Chinese frontier, a person stepped into one of the few remaining preserves in the modern world untouched by all the hallmarks of Western trade and culture. Such contrariness made for fascinating exploration.

Yet China under Mao raised many questions which were troubling. At the same time that I found myself absorbed in the conundrum of China's unique revolutionary experiment, I was also made uneasy by the unexplained refusal of the Chinese people themselves to open up to their "foreign friends." There seemed to be so great a stigma attached to associating with foreigners that almost every Chinese remained aloof and unapproachable except when their official duties brought them into necessary contact with Westerners. One felt as if there was an invisible line drawn between *us* and *them* across which Chinese colleagues would not venture. It was true that guides and officials were tireless and utterly attentive to our every need. We were put up in the finest guest houses and hotels. We were feted with so many banquets that we finally made ardent pleas that such formalities be dispensed with.

Yet, I had the feeling that behind all the hospitality, visitors were only politely tolerated. Our keepers seemed intent on creating a special, artificial environment for us, lest we stumble into the unplanned world of Chinese reality where the revolutionary word had not been made flesh as convincingly as they might have wished us to believe. Instead of heartfelt conversation, we were regaled with endless socialist statistics, "brief-introductions," testimonials, and toasts to "friendship." But the chilly abstraction, "friendship," was hardly an adequate substitute for the real act. Its repeated incantation hung like a pall over our journey, underscoring all the more the chasm that lay between us as foreign visitors and the Chinese people, whom we had theoretically come to meet. This deep ambivalence toward foreigners—perhaps the word "fear" would not even be too strong—often made China seem bleak indeed.

Of course, Chinese culture has traditionally not placed high esteem on the outward expression of emotions. In addition, at that time Americans were still not in the greatest repute in China. The Vietnam War did not end until more than a month after I first arrived. Walls, buildings, and chimneys were still emblazoned with fading slogans inveighing against "American Imperialism and its running dogs." In the back streets of China's less cosmopolitan cities, I would sometimes see mothers protectively grab their children as I passed.

China still seemed not to have made up its mind about how to deal "correctly" (that fine Communist word) with emissaries from the tumultuous world outside. Although the symbols which surrounded us (portraits of Marx, Engels, Lenin, Stalin, and Mao), as well as various slogans and banners, were all clearly of modern vintage, I felt a little as if I were reliving the old days when foreigners were viewed as "barbarians" and "foreign devils"; when the object was to sequester by means of "barbarian management" those foreigners who had managed to penetrate the intricate defense network that imperial China had constructed to keep outsiders at a distance.

It was not that those assigned to squire us through China gave any suggestion of hostility or contempt but simply that they shrank back with frustrating predictability from crucial moments of real contact. Almost every official one encountered seemed to be part of the country's immune system: ready to repel invading foreign organisms before they could establish themselves and infect China with outside influence.

One might have thought the ability to communicate in Chinese an incomparable asset. Being fluent was undeniably helpful in practical matters, but it also served to accentuate the impenetrability of the situation. As long as a person could not converse in the native language, it was only logical to assume that the cause of the blockage was simply linguistic. However, when language was manifestly not the barrier, only one conclusion seemed plausible: the Chinese did not wish to communicate beyond a certain point.

In the end, although I learned a great deal about China in 1975, I left feeling unabsorbable. I recrossed the border to Hong Kong feeling almost wistful because this unusual opportunity to live and work for a short time in China had not yielded the bounteous harvest I had hoped for.

Of all the minor rebuffs I received in my efforts to break into a Chinese reality, one incident remains in my mind.

"Would it be possible to rent a bike?" I asked our head guide soon after arriving in Peking.

"Yes. Well . . . you may try," he replied unenthusiastically. Then, after a pause, he brightened slightly, "Or perhaps you can borrow one from a friend."

Such a reply might sound reasonable, but in Peking at that time it was sheer evasion. The guide, an intelligent and experienced young Party member with a good understanding of what he called "You Americans," did not wish to provoke a direct confrontation by saying "No." Instead, he said, "You may try," knowing full well that any such spontaneous effort was unlikely to succeed. As for "borrowing a bicycle from a friend," one might borrow one from a friend if one *had* a friend, which most visitors in China assuredly did not.

Nonetheless, taking this guide at his word, I decided to conduct an experiment.

"Could you tell me if there is a place that rents bicycles?" I asked one of the young attendants in Chinese at the Inquiry Counter in the main lobby of the Peking Hotel.

"No. No. No place," he said, raising an outstretched palm like a policeman signaling a halt to traffic.

"No place?"

"No place."

"Really?"

"Really."

I retreated to the seventeenth floor, where we were staying.

"Where is *that* shop that rents bicycles?" I asked an attendant.

"Oh, yes, it's down Changan Dongjie."

"What's it near?"

"Well . . ." He reined in. "You better ask at the front desk."

I took the elevator down to the sixth floor, where another group of Americans was lodged.

"Is that bicycle rental shop *far* down Changan Dongjie?" I asked the floor attendant.

"Oh, no. About twenty minutes' walk."

"What's it called?"

"Oh . . ." His whole demeanor changed. "I think it's very, very hot to ride a bicycle," he said and refused to divulge any further details.

Moving back down to the lobby, I headed for the post office in the older wing of the hotel.

"Oh, by the way, how far down Changan Dongjie is the bicycle rental shop?" I nonchalantly asked the young clerk while reaching for the glue bottle to seal some envelopes.

"It's just past the old observatory near the Friendship Store," she replied without looking up.

I hopped a bus.

Getting off across from the Friendship Store, I spotted a small white sign on a shop just off the main thoroughfare. Black characters read BICYCLE RENTAL.

I walked in exhilarated. "I'd like to rent a bicycle," I announced triumphantly to a middle-aged woman standing behind a desk near several young men repairing bicycles. She looked me over for an instant before speaking.

"Where's your certificate?" she finally asked.

"What certificate?"

"Your certificate to rent a bicycle."

"How about this?" I presented my passport.

She examined it.

"No, no." She waved it off. "Certificate. You need a certificate from your embassy to rent a bicycle. Here, like this." She handed me a note written in Chinese on a letterhead from the Embassy of Guyana. "Yes, that's the kind of certificate you need," she added emphatically. As I read the note, she began to clean some grease off her hands with a rag, signaling an end to our negotiations.

"You mean I can't rent a bicycle at this bicycle rental shop unless I work at an embassy?"

"We can't rent you a bicycle. It's a directive."

"Can Chinese rent bicycles here without certificates?"

"You're not Chinese."

"So this foreign friend is going to have to walk all the way back to the Peking Hotel?" I said, smiling.

"Oh, no. No!" She broke into a fit of giggling. "No! No! Take a bus! Foreign friends shouldn't walk. Take bus Number One. It only costs ten fen."

Similarly, requests for people's addresses were repeatedly deflected with references to whole ministries, state farms, or factories, where the chance of contacting a person by phone was nil, and where a personal appearance by a socially inclined foreigner in search of a Chinese employee with whom he had talked only once would have been preposterous and embarrassing.

Suggestions made to get together outside the framework of scheduled events were either sloughed off or ignored. Invitations for an informal chat, a walk, or even the sharing of a meal were either declined on the spot or after the subject had left, when a guide or interpreter would usually approach, saying, "Comrade Li sends word that he is sorry, but he won't be able to. . . ." And so one would surrender, banishing from mind any further efforts to contact "Mr. Li."

Chinese one met were even wary of receiving mail from abroad, lest nosy mailmen and neighboring comrades assume they were conspiring in some foreign anti-Party scheme. In all those years before the Gang of Four fell, I do not know of a single foreign visitor who received a personal letter from a private Chinese citizen. Letters sent to China disappeared into the void along with Mr. Li. It was impossible to know if they were ever received.

It was not just that *some* Chinese were aloof in the presence of foreigners, but virtually all Chinese, even the most expansive people, seemed guarded in how intimate they allowed themselves to become. The idea that a touring "foreign guest" might express even the mildest interest in a Chinese member of the opposite sex, much less have an affair, went so far beyond the pale of possibility that it hardly even occurred to anyone.

Although the itineraries of China tours included a variety of cities all across the country, they could not make up in geographical diversity what they lacked in spontaneity. There was an over-organized sameness to the experience at each factory, work brigade, school, hospital, or dam visited. Unplanned sorties to places not on the schedule won a "foreign guest" grim disapproval from the "responsible member" in charge. Moving through China on these packaged tours, one felt like a piece of luggage on an airport baggage carousel.

A visit to the Peking subway, a stop on many tours of the Chinese capital, remains in my mind as a quintessential example of the kind of controlled contact in which the Chinese specialized.

For most Americans, the mention of a "subway" immediately conjures up images of dirty, overcrowded, graffiti-covered New York City trains bucking and swaying as they transport thousands of gum-chewing, paper-reading, snoozing passengers to and from work. To be in a New York subway is emphatically to be, as the Chinese put it, "among the broad masses."

On this occasion, we filed off our private bus and walked down some stairs to find ourselves alone in a spacious and spotless underground station. The only "broad masses" consisted of three other foreign tours, two from Spain and one from Japan.

For a horrifying moment it occurred to me that perhaps we had been fed into a station built especially for foreign visitors. Then, suddenly, I felt a rush of cool air coming down the tunnel. Noiselessly, a modern subway train filled with Chinese riders glided to a stop. Our phalanx of smiling visitors surged toward the opening doors, eagerly anticipating this commute with the ordinary citizens of Peking.

"No! No! Not our train!" cried an agitated guide just as the first few people began to wedge themselves into a dense crowd of startled strap-hanging Chinese.

Somehow I had already known that this was not *our* train, could not be *our* train. For at that time it was unthinkable that our hosts would allow three herds of "foreign guests" to charge unceremoniously onto a subway car already crammed with unsuspecting Chinese workers. Doubtless the China Travel Service was concerned that we, as guests, not be subjected to anything but the finest treatment, a real tradition in China. But there was also, I think, a deeper apprehension behind their decision to keep foreigners separate. Who knew what might happen if one got in the habit of pouring foreigners into unprepared crowds of Chinese, like a careless scientist mixing volatile chemicals?

When our train finally did arrive, of course there was no mistaking it. It was clean, new, and tastefully decorated with colorful brush paintings and calligraphy. It was also absolutely empty!

Once inside, I was surprised to see two Chinese men in the seat directly behind me.

"Where are you from?" I asked, after allowing a respectful moment to elapse.

"Peking," one of them replied.

Just as I was wondering how these two natives had infiltrated our car, the other added, "We're accompanying some foreign guests. We're with those Japanese electronics technicians." He pointed toward two camera-laden men sitting across the aisle. "We're giving them a bird's-eye view of Peking." His wards sat slumped in their seats, eyes closed, heads bowed over their camera equipment hanging around their necks, bodies swaying limply to the motion of the moving car.

—Even though, in many ways, being in China under Mao and the Gang of Four was suffocating, I could still sense the reasons which seemed to have motivated Mao's attempt to cast a protective membrane around his people. I admired these valiant efforts at the same time that I chafed under their rigidity. As a result, a curious question occurred to me. With such efforts to maintain insularity, why had they let a group such as ours in at all, and how did they intend to deal with the influence that we were casting off around us everywhere we went? For it seemed to me that although we were a "friendly" delegation, we were potentially part of the very problem which the Chinese had been attempting to avoid.

On this trip in 1975, our group of Americans spent three weeks working in the fields of the Dazhai Work Brigade,

Xiyang County, Shanxi Province. Although the village hosted a large variety of visiting delegations at that time, none stayed for more than a day or so, and none actually joined the peasants, as we did in the daily regimen of work.

After we arrived, we were assigned to work at various menial tasks, such as spreading compost, gathering cornstalks, and cultivating nut orchards with the sixth-grade class from the Brigade school. As we worked on Dazhai's terraced fields high up on Tiger Head Mountain, the children's initial reserve gave way to a gregarious cheerfulness. Unlike their elders, who often seemed intimidated by their awareness of the fickle political currents always flowing around them, the children were open and talkative. They provided us with more moments of unguarded contact than all their elders put together. Instead of concocting long, boring speeches or "brief introductions" (often read verbatim and lasting for hours), the children were utterly spontaneous in their curiosity about the West. We talked for hours as we worked. Those peasant children, for whom Peking (not to mention New York or San Francisco) was as far away as the stars, listened with absorption as we told them about America. In the isolation of their remote world, "America" sounded like a strange fantasy. As I watched those disciplined, uncomplaining children, who normally spent half a day at school and half a day in the fields, going about their work with no apparent expectation that things might ever be otherwise, I had ample time to consider how our two worlds would finally approach each other. Often I would stand back for a moment, look past them down the terraced, severely eroded valley toward their cave houses, and wonder what would happen if and when my world began to flood into China.

The truth was, though, that the process of cross-cultural pollination had already begun, even if on a scale that was hardly noticeable. The trickle had not yet become a torrent. Nonetheless, the children eyed our clothes, our shoes, our watches, and above all our cameras with curiosity and, sometimes, with a faint hint of longing.

Although most of them were familiar with ordinary cameras, none of them had ever seen a Polaroid camera work. One of our group members, a tall pale boy whom the children had ungraciously dubbed The Big White Turnip, had such a camera. Because of the anticipated reaction, he did not bring it into the fields until the last day.

When he first started loading it during a work break, the kids seemed unimpressed. They did mug and clown around as he raised it for the first shot, but general calm prevailed. It was not until the first moist print emerged from the bottom of the camera that the children broke ranks. As the milky image slowly sharpened before their eyes, the children gathered in a hushed knot around The Big White Turnip. For them, the delivery of that photograph from his American camera was more impressive than the process of birth itself; and when they realized that he was actually going to give away the photographs, pandemonium broke loose. The social chemistry high up on that remote mountainside changed instantly. The children, who until that moment had been models of obedience and politeness, began to mob The Big White Turnip, thrusting their dusty hands forward as they pushed and shoved toward the still-damp print.

The children seemed possessed. They did not quiet down until one of the larger boys had conclusively seized the print and run with it to the other side of the terrace. Only then did they consent to re-arrange themselves so that the next exposure could be taken. But even when lined up, they stood tensely like runners awaiting the report of the starting gun. As soon as the shutter clicked, they immediately sprang forward and charged The Big White Turnip with such force that he was compelled to retreat.

After three or four more shots, he had backed right up against a stone terrace wall that dropped precipitously fifteen feet to another field below. Unable to get all the advancing kids in each frame, The Big White Turnip began to shoot randomly just to finish the film. The last few photos were filled with nothing more than the heads of several of the more aggressive children.

The uproar over this wondrous piece of technology did not subside until the last photo had been shot and grabbed. Those children who succeeded in procuring prints for themselves were exultant; those empty-handed were crestfallen. They hopped around the photographic battleground on their haunches like oversized frogs examining each bit of Polaroid litter—the box, the instructions, and the film's plastic backing —hoping to discover an overlooked print.

My American colleagues and I stood mutely aside and watched what our collective American expertise had unleashed. Most of us were stunned, caught off balance by our own power over our small work mates. Although no one could quite put his or her finger on it, we all seemed to share an intuitive sense that something ignoble had just transpired, that the sudden unveiling of a miraculous and seductive American toy had somehow violated our relationship with those children, who had actually become our friends. Like a conjurer who suddenly surprises a crowd of unsuspecting people with an unfathomable act of magic, we had separated ourselves unfairly from the children.

Walking down the mountain that last day with my mattock over my shoulders, I recall wondering how the Chinese would ever keep their minds on their revolution and maintain a belief in their own strength if they were constantly subjected to such distracting demonstrations of Western consumer prowess.

On trips to China since 1975, I have witnessed countless more "Polaroid incidents." Communicating with instant photos is, after all, a tempting form of instant contact between two people who are linguistically cut off. Handing a stranger a photo of himself sixty seconds after exposing it promises instant gratification to both parties. But each time the shutter clicks and the print is ground out the bottom of the camera by its small Polaroid motor, the chemistry between China and the West changes another almost immeasurable bit.

Mao Zedong had a second sense about this chemistry. It was certainly true that Western imperialism had a serious economic and political impact on China during Mao's early years. But far subtler was the way in which foreign domination, as well as the foreign presence, crippled the Chinese sense of their own self-esteem. The "wealth and power" of the West may have been exemplary for some of China's earlier reformers who looked forward to China's modernization. But to others it was an intimidating and discouraging sign of China's backwardness and ineptness, so overwhelming and so impressive that it seemed futile to struggle against it.

Mao reacted to this sense of despair. He was a participant in the early days of student unrest just before and after World War I as China's first politically active generation came of age. He was part of the whole movement that turned on traditional Chinese life and thought with vengeance, and turned toward the West for "science and democracy," as the slogan of the day had it. But as others went abroad to study, more and more drawn to Western ideas and styles of life, Mao stayed home, steadfast in his conviction (in spite of his interest in Marxism) that the primacy of things Chinese must somehow survive this new infatuation with the West.

By the time Mao died, the identity of the Chinese people seemed firmly anchored in Mao's nationalist Marxism. Mao Zedong Thought had become the new lingua franca of China. In spite of the nightmarish, claustrophobic aspects of his Thought, Mao had succeeded in nurturing a new Chinese persona and a new Chinese sense of pride. The task had taken decades but was partially responsible for uniting and galvanizing China after a long period of anarchy and privation.

It was probably true that some of China's new sense of pride was only a propagandistic sleight of hand designed to create the illusion of strength where little existed. But it was undeniable that China had in fact "stood up," as Mao triumphantly announced from the Gate of Heavenly Peace in 1949. China's people seemed to have regained a new sense of their own integrity, not as Confucian Chinese, nor as Nationalist Chinese, but as revolutionary Communist Chinese. Mao had succeeded in gathering up the energy of his people and refocusing it inward.

By dint of its own human will power and energy rather than borrowed know-how and capital, China was going to spring forth on the international scene as a modern nation. The process might violate all Western theories of economic development and industrial growth, but if it worked (and Mao never doubted that it would) China would have executed a stunning end run around both capitalism and imperialism, liberating itself not only politically and economically, but psychologically as well.

On October 6, 1976, shortly after the death of Mao, the Gang of Four (four politically militant heirs to Mao's throne, including his wife Jiang Qing), were arrested, a date of such significance to the Chinese that they now refer to it in a way that reminds one of the line of demarcation between B.C. and A.D.

When I returned to China for a short trip in 1978, it was like entering a different country.

I could feel the change in the glances and smiles of people walking in the street. Conductors, hotel personnel, shopkeepers, waitresses, had begun to chat with foreigners. Officials at factories and communes spoke without prepared texts and answered questions in a much less evasive manner. Americans used to making oblique apologies for their heritage found that far from being objects of disapprobation, they were now revered emissaries from a promised land.

By 1979, Chinese began to approach foreigners in the streets, often expressing interest in Western life and culture. After initial contact, many made dates to meet again, and began to pour out stories of their past lives and their hopes for the future.

Soon many were turning toward the West with ravenous appetites—particularly urban intellectuals who had been returning by the millions from the countryside (whence they had been sent "to learn from the workers, peasants, and soldiers"). They welcomed renewed contact with Westerners with thinly disguised delight.

A director of a Peking mental hospital who was trained in San Francisco in the 1940s spoke openly of Sigmund Freud when I visited his hospital and acknowledged that mental disease was not always an affliction caused by "class oppression."

An editor of one of China's foreign-language magazines showed up for tea with some friends of mine at the Peking Hotel and was so talkative that they almost missed their dinner engagement.

A young judge's assistant inquired about the cost of apartments and availability of jobs in the U.S. and then unabashedly told me of his desire to leave China.

"Experts," the outcasts of the previous period, were rehabilitated. "Reds," the politically radical youths who came of age during the Cultural Revolution, vanished from public view. At least in the cities, many Chinese youths began to turn away from politics and toward modernization and their own individual fulfillment. At the same time, personal relations began to be officially reappraised as a legitimate focus of life. Youth publications discussed courtship and marriage in detail and concluded that there was even a place in life for "romantic love," an admission which would have been an apostasy under the Gang of Four. Everywhere a foreigner looked, people seemed to be seeking expertise, excitement, self-expression, and even self-indulgence. In a few short years, the ambience of urban China had been transformed.

Wall posters criticizing the government and calling for "science and democracy," went up in Peking. Underground newspapers proliferated. Citizens whose reputations and careers had been destroyed by the Gang of Four staged sit-ins at Party headquarters. Disco parties, where foreigners socialized and danced with Chinese, were approved. Chinese women began to have their hair permanented and to wear dresses and even make-up. Prostitution, considered all but eradicated, reappeared.

Youths stopped tourists in the streets to speak English, bum cigarettes, buy foreign exchange, or convince them to part with their pocket calculators and tape recorders, which brought healthy resale prices on the Chinese black market. Western goods of all kinds became the rage. Even taxi drivers expressed a preference for Mercedes-Benz and Toyotas over Red Flag limousines or Shanghai-brand sedans.

For foreigners whose first associations were with Mao's China, the China of Deng Xiaoping was positively disorienting. Newly arrived American correspondents no longer found Peking so monotonous and enigmatic. China began to appear not only more friendly but more intelligible. In fact, it was curious to watch how sympathy for China grew as its people appeared to become more like ourselves.

Maoist China had never made much sense to the Western press. But as crime, dissent, prostitution, corruption, unemployment, and inflation—all those problems which we as Westerners knew back home—became acknowledged Chinese problems as well, one could feel the sense of understanding spread among the previously skeptical Western community.

No one asked, or seemed to care, where all those Chinese who had once rallied against the iniquities of Western imperialism and vociferously called for putting "politics in command" had disappeared to. Most Westerners appeared content to assume that this part of China's past had evaporated into thin air, and none too soon.

In the cities where China's educated elite held forth, there was great jubilation. It was, however, virtually impossible to know how China's vast peasantry was reacting to this sudden change. In many ways, they were now more cut off from China's cities than urban intellectuals were from the West, which was now expressing such great relief and satisfaction at China's turn toward "moderation." Almost all Westerners seemed to exhort China onward in a way that suggested their own political narcissism. They seemed more fascinated by their reflection now staring back at them from the Chinese looking glass than by what remained unfamiliarly Chinese.

For the most part, American and other foreign businessmen, diplomats, students, and reporters flooding back into China seemed thankful to be able to relax their guard and not have to deal with militant activists or troublesome socialist values. Their enthusiasm over the new China was tinged with not a little relief and self-congratulation, as if the final vindication had been theirs.

Leaders of the Chinese Communist party watched with a mixture of pride and uneasiness as their people began conjugating with Westerners and experimenting with their newly granted freedoms. Often these leaders seemed unsure how to control and respond to the carnival of new ideas and forces which they had unleashed around them. After so many years, there were few who felt self-assured in such virgin territory.

For instance, prior to his visit to America, Vice-Premier Deng Xiaoping upheld the right of Chinese to air grievances and plaster Democracy Wall with critical posters. In a remark credited to him in early 1979, the *People's Daily* editorialized: "Let the people say what they wish. The heavens will not fall." But by the beginning of 1980, pressured by opposing factions within the Central Committee, and perhaps harboring new doubts of his own, Deng became increasingly irritated with the seemingly limitless capacity of his people to dissent from the tutelage of their Party.

There were arrests and trials of some of the more militant dissidents, such as Wei Jingshen, an employee at the Peking Zoo who had called China's leaders "autocratic careerists" and the dictatorship of the proletariat "despotic." Wei justified his actions by saying, "Criticism cannot possibly be nice and appealing to the ear. . . . The constitution gives people the right to criticize leaders because they are human beings, not deities." Wei received a sentence of fifteen years in jail.

Next, the government ordered Democracy Wall moved to an obscure park and required the registration of all future authors of wall posters. Then Deng himself called for the removal of the clause in China's recently promulgated constitution that guaranteed citizens the right to express themselves publicly through wall posters.

While the Chinese government was searching for the correct means of tempering this unfamiliar wave of domestic dissent and protest, it was also granting potentially subversive exit permits to thousands of students for study abroad. In addition, by 1980, the stream of Western tourists visiting China was augmented by growing contingents of foreign teachers and students who were allowed to fan out across China to live, work, and study. Each of these foreigners acted like a minuscule time-release capsule beneath the skin of China. Without malicious intentions, each was releasing new ideas, and thus new expectations, among those with whom they came in contact.

Many officials with whom I talked were not unaware of the contradictory implications of their policies. Still, taken as a whole, it almost appeared as if the Chinese government was in a struggle with itself. The leadership seemed to oscillate, uncertain how finally to resolve the two opposing tendencies inherent in their program of modernizing China: to protect China while opening up and developing the country with Western expertise and resources.

Being in China again as the tide changed after Mao's death and Westerners came back into fashion was both wonderful and unsettling. Far from feeling quarantined as I once had, I now felt much more a part of China, albeit an American part. No longer the passive observer I had once been, I quite unexpectedly found myself involved as an active agent of change, part of the powerful new invasion from the West. Yet, agreeable as it always is to be admired, I found myself becoming uncharacteristically cautious with Chinese acquaintances.

The tables had been turned. Again and again I noticed myself expressing concern to Chinese friends over the increasingly intense liaison which I saw developing between *us* and *them*, lest China again be derailed from its commitment to honor itself and simply spin off on a tangential infatuation with things foreign. Potentially at stake, it seemed to me, was the integrity of China's national identity.

There was something unsettling about the suddenness and totalism of the Chinese change of attitude. The discontinuity had come so quickly and was so great, it was difficult to believe that the structural foundations beneath the new policies could have any strength. If China's opposition to all that the U.S. and the West stood for had finally proven so mutable, what about this new infatuation? Was it possible that the pendulum would soon swing back? Although it may be a cliché to say that love and hate are merely opposite sides of the same emotion, it was still far from clear in my own mind how such passionate opposition could so fluidly be converted into such convincing admiration without the identity of the Chinese people suffering a severe shock. Whereas China once had impressed me with its unparalleled protectionism against the disruptive inroads of the outside world, now it seemed to border on the careless.

Of course, reversals in official policy are not unique to the Chinese. But what made this particular Chinese metamorphosis troubling was the ways in which it seemed to fit into an old historical pattern. Once before, in the period starting just after World War I, China's intelligentsia had sought their country's salvation in Western "science and democracy." Western ideas and styles came very much into vogue. Thousands of young students went abroad to study, and some never came home again. Many of those who did were so changed by their lives in the Western world that they found it difficult to readjust to the backwardness of their homeland. Even idealists devoted to the reconstruction of China often had become so distant from the problems of rural China and its peasantry that they were like foreigners in their own land. They remained in the relative sophistication of China's urban enclaves, more isolated from the mass of peasants who made up the vast majority of their own country than from the outside world. As a result, the division between the cities and the countryside, which had always been a stark one in China, became even starker.

Having a peasant background of his own (albeit, from a "rich peasant" family), Mao had an almost instinctive distrust of China's urban intelligentsia. Their preoccupation with foreign ideas and lifestyles impressed him as a diversion from the main task at hand: the revolutionary transformation of China's peasantry. Mao's genius, almost forgotten with the debunking of the Gang of Four, was not only that he recognized China's "peasant problem" as the crux of the matter, but that he had the fortitude to try to deal with it. So little regard did Mao have for Western ways that during his whole lifetime he went abroad only twice. Both trips were made to the Soviet Union in the 1950s, relatively late in his life. Although interested in keeping abreast of world affairs, Mao was never personally drawn toward the West as many of his foreign-educated comrades were. He was emphatic that China should remain Chinese.

If China's sense of itself was too one dimensional and rigid during the last decades of Mao's life, after his death and the fall of the Gang of Four it moved in the opposite direction until it became fragmented and China seemed to wobble on its cultural political axis, as if a stabilizing gyroscope within was slowly losing rpm's.

Now, with Mao debunked and Bob Hope soft-shoeing on the Great Wall, it is not at all clear what new and cohesive force will give unity and direction to China's one billion people, so that they will not, like mercury hitting the floor, splatter off to all points of the compass. The image of "a sheet of loose sand" used by Sun Yat-sen to describe China more than fifty years ago is still an apt one.

Soon after Deng Xiaoping made his historic journey to the U.S. in the winter of 1979, just such a dispersion of purpose did become noticeable as the shock waves of Western influence once again began to roll across China.

The new China that I saw as I walked through the streets of China's major cities seemed at once exhilarated and disoriented by the change in "political line." With Mao gone, there was no other single man or even a corpus of thought which could provide China with its previous singularity of direction. Instead, an unsteady patchwork of alternatives was springing up all around me. For the Chinese in this book, this change came as a great relief, opening a whole new range of previously forbidden political, commercial, artistic, or simply lifestyle possibilities. Presented with such a new latitude, many Chinese quickly began experimenting with their lives in a way that undoubtedly would have mortified Mao and the

Gang of Four. Like their leaders, whose odyssey through America in 1979 is chronicled in some of the sections which follow, these new post-Mao Chinese plunged forward in search of the "wealth and power"—not to speak of the pleasures—of the West.

Peking

The incandescent lights over Wangfujing, one of Peking's main commercial thoroughfares, cast dappled orange shadows through the leaves of the sycamore trees onto the sidewalks below.

Bicycles whirr down the street in the warm evening air, past the darkened tomblike buildings of the *People's Daily* and the Peking Number One Department Store.

Turning right at the Four Unities Hair Salon, which now displays photos of elegantly coiffed Western models, one passes the East Wind Movie Theater and enters Goldfish Alley, one of the thousands of narrow *hutongs* which comprise the dark back streets of Peking. Although it is only eight o'clock at night, Goldfish Alley is empty of traffic except for a worn wood cart pulled by two thin horses.

Down the alley, a small knot of people, who stand in the half-light shed by a bare bulb, squeeze to one side to let the cart pass.

Drawing near, one can make out the faces of four young men. They laugh in unison and disappear into a doorway from which the sounds of music and voices emerge. This is the Peace Café.

Suddenly the screen door opens. A young man wearing a long, English-style trench coat rakishly buckled at the waist, and a crumpled felt fedora, emerges from the café. He pauses a moment, letting his eyes adjust to the darkness, and then strides across the alley to the neighborhood public latrine, which fills the air with the smell of stale urine. Although it is a seasonal autumn night, he walks with his hands thrust deep into his pockets and his head bent down, as if fighting against a bitter winter wind.

Coming out of the rest room, he nervously lights a cigarette, illuminating a round, impish face flushed red from drinking. His upper lip sports a fuzzy moustache not yet ample enough to need trimming. He looks to be in his early twenties.

This is Wang Zaomin, or Benefit-the-People Wang. He is a soldier in the People's Liberation Army as well as a procurer of women.

From the chin up he looks like a gangster. From his neck to his knees he seems like an Englishman who has just stepped out of his neighborhood pub into the London fog. But below his knees, where his army pants emerge to meet his khaki sneakers, he looks Chinese. His costume—fedora, trench coat, and army uniform—creates the illusion of a man who has been cut in thirds and pasted back together. Compared to the other youths who stand in the alley in their blue jackets, work pants, and Mao caps, Wang Zaomin looks utterly alien.

In a moment, a young woman holding a small purse in both hands emerges from the café and walks over to Wang. Although dressed in a shapeless factory uniform, she wears glossy red lipstick and has hair that cascades seductively down over her shoulders, an unusual coiffeur for a Chinese woman. She is Wu Guiming, or Precious Name Wu.

Benefit-the-People Wang beckons her to follow him as two foreign men leave the café. They walk quickly toward the refuge of a dark niche in a wall just past the latrines. Once there, they converse in low tones, looking ill at ease.

Just then, a car slowly works its way down Goldfish Alley, filling the dark niche with glaring light. Comrade Wu turns her back to the car. The two Western men twist their heads down and to the side in that manner affected by handcuffed mobsters as they pass batteries of press photographers on their way to jail. But Wang stands his ground. Feet planted slightly apart, hands behind his back, he turns directly into the glaring light as if he were Edward G. Robinson facing down the heat.

"Whatever happens," says Wang, turning back to the two

foreigners once the car has passed, "you must return the *xiao mei mei* [literally, "little sister"] by twelve P.M."

The two foreigners nod without speaking.

"Where are you going to take her?" asks Wang with nervous concern. "If you don't have a car, it can be inconvenient. You know that they won't let you into the hotels."

The foreigners nod. But Wang's apprehensions seem unallayed by this acknowledgment. Since he is speaking in Chinese, he is not certain the foreigners understand what he is saying to them.

"How much do you want?" one foreigner finally asks.

There is a long pause. Comrade Wu turns away from the conversation to face the wall.

"One hundred yuan [$60.00]," says Wang, taking a long drag on his cigarette. It comes out sounding more like a question than a statement. His voice quavers.

"Oh no! Much too much," says one of the foreigners. "We've heard that Overseas Chinese get it for fifteen yuan."

"OK. How much then? You say."

"Twenty-five."

"Thirty."

"OK. Thirty," says Wang with relief.

One of the foreigners reaches for his wallet. He holds it out into the alleyway to catch the dim light from the café entrance. He extracts three ten-yuan bills from a colorful bouquet of credit cards and hands the money to Wang.

Wang turns to Precious Name Wu. Having stuffed some of the money into his trench coat pocket, he furtively slips her the rest.

"OK, OK," says Wang, summoning up a little hasty fraternity to close out the deal. "Well, we've made good friends." He shakes hands with the foreigners, then turns and walks back down the alley toward a group of youths who still stand out in front of the café.

One of the "youths," a term which, because of its virtuous

connotations in China, hardly seems suitable in this case, wears a drooping handlebar moustache. His hair is shaggy and long and reaches down below his collar. He is dressed in bell-bottom trousers (called horn pants here in China), and a Count Dracula–style black cape.

Benefit-the-People Wang gives a quick salute to this kindred spirit and steps back inside the café.

In order to enter the Peace Café tonight, one must navigate around a pool of vomit that some "youth" has dispatched right onto the threshold between the two ancient stone lions which guard the door.

Inside, a dense cloud of cigarette smoke mutes the harsh glare that a row of fluorescent lights casts on folding chairs and tables covered with plastic cloths. The two rooms of the café overflow with young men and women. The sound of their voices is loud.

By the entranceway to the second room is an ugly masonry fish pond, the home of several sluggish carp, which two customers have just caught and lifted out of the water with their bare hands.

Across from the fish tank, two other youths in brightly colored form-fit shirts sit around a large portable combination radio and hi-fi cassette player, reminiscent of those that young black men carry at high volume through the streets of New York. Plastic cassette boxes are conspicuously arrayed around them on the tabletop. They play a continuous program of Chinese music from Hong Kong like DJ's at a discotheque.

Benefit-the-People Wang sits down at a table inside the café with a group of other youths, who eat cake and potato salad, and drink a mixture of orange pop and Peking-brand beer, a popular Chinese version of English shandy.

"These are all my good friends," says Wang, as if he had just introduced the Standing Committee of the Chinese Communist Party's Central Committee.

He raises a glass of pop and beer.

"*Ganbei!* [bottoms up]" he says authoritatively and gulps down a whole tumbler of the vile mixture.

"I come here every night," Wang says proudly. "I leave my People's Liberation Army cap and red insignias at home, and come on down." He grins, and with his thumbs and forefingers reaches up to the lapels of his khaki army jacket, making a pantomime gesture as if to pluck loose his army I.D. insignias and defrock himself right there in the Peace Café.

Sitting and drinking with this jolting parody of a Chinese revolutionary warrior before me at a table covered with empty beer bottles, I find it hard to believe that only a few years ago, PLA soldiers were so hallowed that foreigners were told it was inappropriate to photograph them, much less consort with them at an after-hours café.

"Come here! Look here!" says Wang all of a sudden, grabbing the head of a handsome-faced young man who sits at the next table. "I want you to meet my friend New Nation Li."

Wang holds the grinning head of his friend by the hair and chin, and does not release it until the grinning comrade and I have shaken hands.

"I want you to look at this guy." Wang grabs his head again and yanks it around by the hair until he has presented me with a perfect profile. "Do you think my friend looks Chinese? Don't you think he'd even be considered handsome abroad? Maybe he'd make a movie star," he adds, unceremoniously dropping his comrade's head again.

His friend, who is attired in a silken shirt and a well-tailored, gray Western suit with tight-fitting bell-bottom pants and pointed black shoes, appears pleased with this rave evaluation of his looks.

"Yes, in many ways he does look like he might come from abroad."

"Do you really think so?" inquires Wang, delighted that Li should have provoked such acclaim from a foreigner.

"I got this suit from my father," offers Li with a cheerful, toothy smile. "He's a general."

"Doesn't he mind you dressing up this way?"

"He doesn't know. He's always away."

"What about other people?"

"No one bothers me. Everything is different now. Since the Gang of Four, we can do as we please," he says proudly, as if he, in all his Western sartorial splendor, were the living embodiment of China's Fifth Modernization.

"My father is also some kind of a general," adds Benefit-the-People Wang diffidently, taking another hearty gulp of his drink, leaving a ring of beer and pop on his moustache and upper lip like a scum line on a drained tub. "I should say 'was' a general. It's all so boring. Now he's teaching at some army college. When I graduated from middle school and couldn't get a job, he got me into the army . . . 'through the back door.'" Wang smiles with satisfaction at the thought.

Wang uses the phrase "to go through the back door" (*zou hou men*) with an irreverence that is surprising. Until recently, such an admission was tantamount to confessing yourself a counterrevolutionary. The expression is still a euphemism for anyone who succeeds in getting a good apartment, gains entrance to a good school or university, obtains a decent job, or otherwise receives special treatment because of the intercession of an influential friend or family member. For Wang to sit here in this den of Peking iniquity, boasting with insouciance that his father got him into the army "through the back door," is something akin to the Reverend Billy Graham suddenly announcing that he has joined a cult of Satan worshippers.

"I love foreigners," he announces cheerfully. "Hey, Li! Tell my friend here about all the foreigners we know."

Unable to attract Li's attention, Wang continues the testimonial himself. "Li and I are really good friends with this man from the Pakistani Embassy. We knew the Dutch ambassador before he went home, and we also have some African friends."

Indeed, it appears as if some of Wang's "African friends" are even now in the café. In the next room several tall black men with bushy Afro hairdos and colorful African shirts sit at a table, drinking beer and eating cake.

"We get them anything they want," boasts Wang. "A lot of them are students, and they get lonely here. So we introduce girls to them. Right, Li?" Wang leans back to the next table and fraternally grabs Li's hand, a common sign of friendship among men in China.

"Right," says Li agreeably.

"There are a lot of girls here who like to meet foreigners. Maybe you'd like to meet some pretty girls," says Wang with a sly smile.

"Sure," I say, not certain whether or not I have heard him correctly, since Wang speaks no English, and by this time he has begun speaking Chinese with a slur.

The idea that a woman can be procured in China is a startling one. And that one can be procured through a People's Liberation Army soldier still seems almost too fantastic to believe.

But tonight there are, in fact, several young women drifting around the café dressed in a brazen Western fashion. Instead of wearing baggy blue, gray, or khaki uniforms, they wear tailored slacks and colorful, tight-fitting sweaters. Several wear their hair in bangs or hanging loosely down their backs. Their lips, covered with bright crimson lipstick, contrast sharply with their pale skin and jet black hair.

One young woman with a saucy smile and stylishly bobbed hair, and wearing a tight blue sweater, has been cruising around the room all evening, stopping at different tables to allow various swains to give her quick pecks on the cheek, something I have never seen in China before.

"By eighteen, a lot of these girls have started playing around," says Wang, surveying the scene with satisfaction. "They're bored. They can't get a job. There are a lot of young people unemployed now. They get out of middle school, and since there are not enough jobs, they can't get assigned anywhere." Wang uses the word *fen pei*, which means "to be assigned to a job by your school or unit," the only way to come by work in China. "They don't have anything to do, so they come to places like this."

Suddenly, over by the fish pond there is a commotion. The room immediately quiets down as everyone turns to see what is happening.

Two young women are scuffling in the corner. One is trying to grab the other but is meeting with resistance.

"The younger girl comes here all the time," whispers Wang without taking his eyes off the struggle. "The older girl is her sister."

Before the altercation has gone on too long, a group of young people surround the two girls and slowly maneuver the raging battle toward the door and out into Goldfish Alley.

"The older girl doesn't like her young sister to be in places like this," adds Yang Yan, Swallow Yang, a young woman who is also sitting at our table. "It's too disorderly. Their parents don't approve either, so they send the sister here to get her."

The sight of these two brawling females here in the Peace Café is both horrifying and electrifying. The fight before us seems to suggest the magnitude of the change which is gripping Chinese society. Whereas not long ago the public display of such naked emotions and lack of discipline while foreigners were present would have been inconceivable. Now the people here seem to take it in stride, no longer trying to hide such human frailties as if they would irrevocably besmirch the purity of the revolution.

"Do your parents approve of your coming here?" I ask, turning to Swallow Yang.

"No, but I don't tell them where I'm going." She casts a quick knowing look at one of her girlfriends. "I just say I'm going for a walk or to the movies."

"Aren't you ever afraid that the Public Security Bureau will come in here sometime and . . ."

"The police haven't bothered us here yet," Wang interrupts, using the rather pejorative term *jingcha*, or police, rather than the official and more acceptable term *Gunganbu*, Public Security Bureau. "The only thing the police don't like is when people fight and steal things."

He has another sip of his drink.

"*He* is a good fighter," says Wang, gesturing proudly over toward New Nation Li. Li smiles a gracious acknowledgment.

"If they catch you fighting with a knife, they'll put you in jail for three years. Then, when they let you out, they won't give you a job. That's the real trouble. But I've never gotten caught," concludes Li triumphantly.

Wang hails the waitress and orders more beer, some ice cream sundaes, and a plateful of miniature hot dogs, which appear to be particularly fashionable here at the café.

"You eat hot dogs all the time in the United States, don't you?" asks Swallow Yang, who sits next to three other girls. They all wear lipstick. One is smoking a cigarette. Swallow Yang wears a turtleneck sweater under her uniform jacket and a strange pair of trousers that look as if they might once have been stretch ski pants.

Out of the breast pocket of her blue cotton jacket dangles a small, red, pendantlike object on a string. Since many young Chinese wear plastic pins indicating their place of work or sports club, there is nothing particularly unusual about such adornments, except this is the first time I have seen one that hangs rather than being affixed by a pin.

I ask her if I can see it.

As she unfastens the pendant and hands it to me, she smiles in a way that seems to mix embarrassment with pride.

INCABLOC—SHOCK PROTECTED, say yellow letters embossed on a red plastic background. It is a throw-away tag from an imported wristwatch.

"I found it in the street," says Swallow Yang as I hand it back to her. "Pretty, isn't it?"

By now the beer, ice cream sundaes with chocolate sauce, and miniature hot dogs have arrived. Since there are no other hands at the table reaching for wallets, I pull mine out of my hip pocket to pay for the order. As I open it up, pandemonium breaks loose. For an instant it occurs to me that maybe the other comrades are protesting the fact that I am paying. But no! It turns out that Benefit-the-People Wang and New Nation Li have spotted some unfamiliar currency inside my wallet, some foreign exchange, key to procuring such foreign-made treasures as Parliament and Marlboro cigarettes, Time, Newsweek, and Coca-Cola (whose colorful red and white logo has already been pirated for use in China on several other locally made products, such as playing cards). Of course, Chinese themselves cannot buy these foreign products because they do not possess foreign currency.

"Hey! What's this one? Is it American?" asks Wang, reaching into my wallet and extracting a twenty-dollar bill, more money than many of these youths make in a month.

"Let me see that other one," says another young man, who, in spite of the heat and smoke, is wearing a zipped-up leather jacket. He says it has been issued to him by the air force, where he is a trainee mechanic.

"Can this one buy foreign cigarettes?" he asks, smiling and feeling a ten-dollar note from Hong Kong.

Then, reaching into his baggy pants like a magician about

to perform a trick, Benefit-the-People Wang produces a gold-cased European watch complete with an expensive leather strap. He dangles it out over the table for all to see while the foreign currency samples make their rounds.

"My friends gave me this," he proclaims with bravado, though without being specific about who these friends might be. He takes a swig of beer and pop. "Another friend gave me some American money. And do you know what I did with it?" he continues. "I walked into the Peking Hotel, went straight to the counter, bought some foreign cigarettes, and they didn't even catch me."

I find myself conjuring up the vision of a crimson-faced Benefit-the-People Wang striding into the marble splendor of the Peking Hotel lobby among all the "foreign guests," wearing his caved-in fedora, mysterious trench coat, khaki pants, and sneakers, confidently incognito in his Western disguise.

I am savoring this unlikely hallucination when Wang adds, "Chinese aren't supposed to go in there. You know that, don't you?" He looks at me sternly. "But I just breezed in; I like foreign cigarettes a lot."

By now it is almost 10 P.M. The overhead fluorescent lights blink twice, signaling closing time. After finishing up the food and drink on the table, we rise and follow scores of Chinese youths out of the café.

In Goldfish Alley, having temporarily shelved his offer to procure women, Wang launches into another promotional scheme.

"Listen," he says in hushed, almost reverential tones as we walk toward Wangfujing. "If you ever get a girl . . . you know"—with both hands, he outlines a large protuberance over the front of his stomach—"I've got some of this medicine that makes it come out with just one whiff."

He stops walking.

"Just one whiff." He looks up at me with squinting eyes.

"One whiff, and"—this time, he sweeps the backs of his hands down from his chest to his thighs as if he were brushing something off his jacket— "and out it comes!" For an instant he stands silently, like a preacher who has just made a dramatic point which needs time to sink in.

"I have five hits," he continues. "Actually, I've already used one, so I only have four. I got this *xiao mei mei* pregnant, so I had to give her one."

We begin walking again. We have just reached Wangfujing when Wang stops once more, this time in front of a propaganda poster, each character written in white on a placard with red background. LONG LIVE THE CHINESE COMMUNIST PARTY it proclaims.

Wang stands with his back to it, cocks his head to one side, and turning both palms upward in a gesture of futility, says, "What could I do? I couldn't go to the hospital. They would have given her a whole lot of lectures and gotten her in trouble with her family and workplace."

It is considered extremely bad form for an unmarried girl to become pregnant in China. While there are still numerous stories of single girls who have needed abortions being harassed at hospitals, one young woman later told me that it is now possible to get an abortion quietly "through the back door." The prerequisite? A payoff to the doctor.

"You want to know something?" Wang asks as we once again resume walking. "If a single woman gets pregnant three times, they send her to jail. Do you believe that? Well, it's true. So you have to watch where you 'shoot the old cannon [*da pao*].'" He laughs at this old Chinese expression for sexual intercourse.

"Do you want some girls?" Wang asks, returning to the inevitable subject. "I'll tell you what. Come back to the café tomorrow at seven-thirty, and I'll have some *xiao mei meis* there. Pretty ones."

"Do you fool around with girls a lot?"

"Yeah." He almost shrugs the question off. "But it's not that interesting. Hey, why don't you come over for a visit? You could come to Li's house. Here, Li, write your address down."

New Nation Li gives his usual compliant smile to Wang's suggestion that he offer his house up for a meeting with foreign journalists. It is not until Wang hands him a pad and pencil to write down his address that he protests. Surprisingly enough, his protestations have nothing to do with any apprehensions about meeting foreigners in the inner sanctums of his house. In fact, the thought seems to please him.

"No. No. You do it," says Li, waving off the pad. "You know how ugly my characters are. I can hardly write." He laughs as if his failure to learn how to write were itself a significant accomplishment.

"I never did much studying in school," he adds by way of explanation. "But I was a good fighter. I always won."

When Wang presses the small pad on him anyway, Li slowly writes his address in the cramped and graceless script of so many young Chinese who have spent virtually no time in school over the last fifteen years.

The following night, from fifty yards down the alley, I spot Benefit-the-People Wang standing outside the café with New Nation Li. Li is wearing his gray Western suit and pointed black shoes, although he has substituted a sleeveless undershirt for the nylon dress shirt beneath his jacket. Unadorned by his trench coat and fedora, Wang wears only his army uniform, minus insignia, and khaki sneakers. It is obvious that both youths have been here awhile, drinking. Wang's face has already turned the bright scarlet of a severe sunburn. As soon as he spots me, he heads in my direction with an outstretched hand in welcome.

"You're too late! Too late," he says immediately, a suggestion of defensiveness in his voice. "The *xiao mei meis* have already left. There were just too many people. So much coming and going . . ." His apologies are effusive.

"But how about tomorrow night? We'll get some more," he offers as consolation. His eagerness to make new promises suggests that he is more interested in being well thought of than in actually producing the *xiao mei meis*. "Anyway, let's go in and have something to drink."

Inside the café, the air is so thick with smoke that it is difficult to breathe. Despite the low visibility, Wang squires us confidently to a table filled with a group who are again introduced as "my friends."

They cordially scurry around the room looking for empty chairs. They are pleased to sit with foreigners, any foreigners, in their passion to be cosmopolitan.

We sit down. The waitress arrives, and Wang sovereignly orders the usual kind of bizarre fare: tonight, beer cum pop, pickled beets, potato salad, cake, and shrimp chips.

Several tables away there is a young man whose appearance immediately distinguishes him from the rest of the café patrons. His black hair is neatly combed down over his forehead so that he looks like a Chinese Julius Caesar. His eyebrows stand out with such prominence that I wonder if he has not either plucked them or touched them up with mascara. He sits alone, head thrown back, and smokes languidly in a stylized manner, as if he were posing for photographs.

"Are there any homosexuals in China?" I ask Wang.

At first, he seems confused. Since I am not exactly sure how homosexuals (if, in fact, they exist here) are referred to, it is hard to tell whether or not he has understood me.

"You know. Men who go with men."

He shows a glimmer of recognition.

"Yes. I see," he says. "There are some old men, foreign men, who come here." But before he can elaborate, our attention is distracted by a drunken soldier who is harassing a young woman.

Having more or less trapped the unwilling female comrade between a table and the wall, the grinning soldier is trying to kiss her. She warns him angrily to stop. He ignores her entreaties. Finally, she shoves him. To prevent himself from toppling over backwards, he grabs at the front of her jacket and tries clumsily to feel her breasts.

"Stop it!" she says again and again, becoming more and more furious. But she cannot dislodge her assailant, who drapes himself over her like a punch-drunk fighter.

"Get out of here!" she cries. Then she hauls off and half hits, half slaps him on the side of the face.

The shocked soldier reels back, allowing the girl to escape. Then, still grinning, he lumbers out the door after her.

This incident is hardly over before a scuffle between two comrades breaks out on the other side of the room. Just as it is about to turn into a punching and swinging free-for-all, a group of friends springs into action and leads the two adversaries off like quarreling dogs.

In fact, the whole café seems to be in constant motion. People are moving from table to table with incredible rapidity, as if they were playing an accelerated version of musical chairs. It is not long before both Wang and Li have disappeared into the other room. It occurs to me that perhaps moving around the room from table to table is the Chinese sitdown equivalent to cutting and double-cutting in Western ballroom dancing.

I am just beginning to enjoy my relative solitude when a young soldier, whose head has been resting inertly on the adjacent tabletop, comes to life.

"What do you do?" asks Brilliant Hu, his eyes half-opened.

"I'm a writer interested in Chinese history," I reply, making my response as succinct as possible for this obviously inebriated inquirer.

"Ahhhh," he says. He takes another gulp of beer and then, losing all body timber, does a slow-motion collapse back to his head-on-top-of-the-table position. Although his body appears lifeless, his eyes are still open.

I have just struck up a new conversation with another young man, Bright Book Huang, at my own table, when I sense a tugging on one of my sleeves. I turn to discover that Comrade Hu has come back to life.

"History. Chinese history. Yes. Good! Good!" he says, not addressing me as much as evaluating my avocation. "I too am interested in Chinese history."

There is no easy way to respond to Hu. Just as I am on the verge of saying something in praise of the greatness and durability of Chinese history, he again collapses onto the tabletop.

Never mind. Back at my own table, Bright Book Huang is interested in pursuing matters other than history.

"So you like girls?" he asks, with a tentative smile on his face. "Would you like to meet a pretty girl?"

I quickly scan the room for Wang, feeling that I may be provoking a turf battle here. But he is down at the far end of the room, puffing feverishly on a cigarette and talking with other "friends."

"Do you have a lot of girlfriends?" I ask Comrade Huang, trying to guide the discussion away from the question of procurement.

"Me?" he asks incredulously, pointing at his nose (the Chinese equivalent of pointing to one's chest to indicate the self). "I don't have even *one* girlfriend. I'm too ugly. None of these girls will even look at me." He laughs, unwounded by the notion of his own modest looks.

Indeed, Bright Book Huang has none of the dashing attributes of, say, New Nation Li. His face is pock-marked and his teeth are crooked. He wears ordinary factory workers' dress; otherwise, he gives an overall impression of being a cheerful, even somewhat earnest person. Hardly the Western stereotype of a pimp or hustler.

"Which of the girls in this room do you think is the prettiest?" He gestures around the room with his arm like a general surveying the troops.

I laugh, not sure what kind of beauty contest Comrade Huang is promoting.

"OK," he says, moving forward on his own initiative. "I'm going to find the prettiest one here and bring her over."

He leaps out of his chair and heads off down the aisle into the smoke.

But it is not Bright Book Huang who finally reappears with the winning beauty queen. It is Benefit-the-People Wang who walks down the aisle between the tables with a young woman in tow.

"This is Golden Thunder Chen," he says while reaching around behind him for an empty chair. She sits down as if she were about to begin a job interview. Benefit-the-People Wang evaporates.

Golden Thunder Chen has short, lusterless, wiry hair that looks as if it might have been singed on curling irons, an accouterment for the permanent waves which are presently sweeping China. She wears a Western-style orange and white polyester shirt. Instead of the standard gray-, blue-, or khaki-colored jacket, she wears a red sweater with a white pattern across the chest. In place of the usual loose cotton trousers that enshroud the torsos and legs of most Chinese women, Golden Thunder wears a pair of form-fitting, tattersall, bell-bottom pants. Although slightly stained, they do indeed single her out as someone special among the other women in the room.

Golden Thunder has perfect pearl-white teeth. Although her skin is marred by several deep acne scars on each cheek, she has a warm and open smile. She shows no suggestion of cynicism or hardness or even of embarrassment at having been so unceremoniously thrust upon a foreigner.

"I like foreigners," she says, breaking the ice, "but I have not had the chance to meet many. I have met only a few men from Arabia. They were very nice."

It is hard to know what she means: whether she has simply chatted with some Arabs or whether she has spent the night with them. Watching her sit primly upright in her seat, both hands modestly in her lap, it is also hard to know what she is feeling. "It's so boring here," she says. "It's exciting to meet people from interesting places like America and Arabia."

At just this moment, Benefit-the-People Wang cruises by again on his way to a table in the other room. He winks but without any suggestion of prurience, and takes a drag on his Golden Horse cigarette, apparently pleased that he has at last been able to produce a *xiao mei mei* for his "foreign friend."

"I can't get a job," continues Golden Thunder Chen. "It's been a whole year since I graduated from middle school. I don't have any money to do anything. I live at home and spend most of my time just hanging around reading books. It's really dull!"

"Are there many other young people who can't get work now?"

"Oh, yes. A lot." She furrows her brow in apparent amazement that such an obvious fact could have escaped anyone's attention. "Since they stopped sending the 'educated youth' to the countryside, there are a lot of people looking for work. So, while I wait, I come down here at night. But even sitting here sometimes gets dull."

I pour some beer and orange pop for Golden Thunder, wondering what fantasies of Western life she harbors in her heart. I look at her plain but friendly face, and wonder if before her present ardor to meet foreigners, she was ever driven by such slogans as "Serve the People with All Your

Heart and Soul" or "Put Politics in Command." It is hard to
know how to broach such a question, especially to a young
woman introduced to a foreigner in this gloomy little café for
purposes which are at best ambiguous.

Golden Thunder sips her drink with grace and then smiles.
Like other characters who emerge during my stay in China,
she seems like a caricature from some perverse drama in
which everyone turns into his or her opposite by the final act.

"I also love to dance. I love to waltz, fox trot, even rock
and roll," she says, emitting a knowing giggle, an acknowledgment of her addiction to the forbidden. "We used to be
able to go to the International Club or to the Nationalities
Cultural Palace to dance if a foreigner would invite us. But
now they won't let us in."

We both sit locked in our own thoughts for a few minutes.

"I like the way Western women make themselves up," says
Golden Thunder, breaking the silence. "I think a woman's
appeal is seventy percent in how she dresses and only thirty
percent in her own face and body," she proclaims as if she
were Diane Von Furstenberg doing a commercial for a new
line of beauty aids.

"Do you like Western clothes?"

"Yes, very much," she replies. "They're so colorful and
beautiful. Now we can get a few new styles which are made
here in China; they're much more plentiful than during the
Gang of Four. But they're mostly for women. Actually, men's
clothes are still really ugly."

She wrinkles up her nose, turns around, and plucks up a
pleat of the shapeless army jacket that the collapsed Brilliant
Hu is wearing. Then she lets it fall back as if she were jetti-
soning a dirty Kleenex.

"Ehhhh!" she says with distaste. "That's all these guys ever
wear."

Feeling Golden Thunder tug on his jacket, Brilliant Hu
stirs from his hibernation. Slowly he turns toward us and with

great deliberation, but perfect articulation, says, "I believe that every country and every people have their own unique traits. It is important for people to preserve their own traits. I do not care for some of the Western clothes and customs that are coming into China."

Golden Thunder is stunned by this sermon, which she has provoked from an apparently sleeping soldier. Although far from sober, Brilliant Hu speaks with such clarity and succinctness that there is no dismissing his words. Rather than appearing as just another decadent youth at the Peace Café, Brilliant Hu's whole demeanor suddenly changes. He now impresses one as the voice of intelligence and patriotic pride.

"These characteristics are good," he continues, showing no malice toward Golden Thunder, even though what he is saying directly contradicts her. "I like my clothes. They are one of the things that is special to us Chinese, as is our unique trait of being friendly to foreigners."

He grabs the front of his jacket to underscore his point. "I don't think we should be bullied by foreigners. I said I was interested in Chinese history." He looks intently at me. "You used to bully us. That wasn't right. And now I don't think you should bring all your fashions and ways here to China. It's not right to have places where people pay to see women take off their clothes in public."

Brilliant Hu's head wobbles slightly on the top of his neck. Then, as though the pull of gravity were a force against which he was incapable of continued resistance, he buckles and slumps back on the table, leaving Golden Thunder and me speechless.

Again the overhead fluorescent lights blink on and off.

Three young men with beet-red faces, arms slung around each other's shoulders, walk past us down the aisle toward the door. Alone, China's Julius Caesar follows them.

Golden Thunder and I keep our seats awhile, waiting for the initial surge of this nouvelle vague of Chinese underground culture to move out onto the street. Then Benefit-the-People Wang appears in the doorway and enters, working his way against the tide of youths on their way out. He signals to Golden Thunder. She rises. We walk out into the darkness.

Outside, Benefit-the-People Wang begins to engage in another of his habitual tête-à-têtes with New Nation Li, this time including Golden Thunder.

"Thank you, Golden Thunder," I say loudly and clearly. "It was pleasant talking with you. I hope I'll see you again."

Wang stops his negotiations for a moment as the import of my words of farewell sink in. Quickly understanding that he has not made a deal between Golden Thunder and me, he seems more relieved than downcast.

"Let's go out to Changanjie together," he proposes cheerfully. We walk away from Goldfish Alley, which is still filled with youths lingering awhile longer before they finally disperse, boarding crowded busses to return home to their dorms and cramped family apartments.

"Hey! I want you to meet some more of my friends," says Wang, presenting a young man whom he introduces as Golden Thunder's brother (doubtless a euphemism, since many of the habitués of the Peace Café call each other brother and sister as if they were members of a secret society), and another youth in a Western suit. Wang extols him as a person who is "really able to take care of business."

We chat idly as we walk down the quiet back streets of Peking.

As we draw under a streetlight on Wangfujing, Wang and his anonymous friends stop. His accomplice in the Western suit pulls out his wallet and extracts a small graduation-style snapshot. A pretty young girl with her hair in a ponytail looks innocently out. The photo bears the inscription: Red Star Photo Shop. Both youths look up suggestively.

"What do you say? Isn't she a beauty?" inquires Wang with the same naïve optimism that has marked the beginning of each of his seemingly endless offers of procurement. "Will you come again tomorrow night?"

Although I am leaving Peking the next day, I nod non-committally, out of deference to his enthusiasm.

"OK. No big deal," says Benefit-the-People Wang as he slips the photo reverently back into the wallet like a rebuked door-to-door salesman.

"No problem." He extends his hand to shake mine. "We're here every night."

It is hard to say just exactly what it was that brought me back again and again to the Peace Café. It was certainly not the promise of Benefit-the-People Wang's *xiao mei meis* or even the excitement. But I found myself somehow drawn to that scene—one possible preview of the future as China opens ever wider to the seductions of the West.

I found myself at once fascinated and repelled by this vanguard of landlocked deviance, which has only just germinated on the fringes of the Chinese Revolution. Of course, on the Richter scale of international decadence, what was happening there in Peking was nothing, no more than an insignificant blip. But within China itself, the very existence of these few youths suggests something far deeper and more significant than even they themselves seem to know.

Professing no lofty ideals of service to the people and demonstrating no political fervor, these "bad eggs," "poisonous weeds," or "contaminated blossoms" are the indicators of Chinese society in the first stages of a cataclysmic change, a change which may alter the face of China in ways which will be as profound as Mao's own revolution.

Though Benefit-the-People Wang and his "friends" had few socialist virtues to recommend them, there was something poignant, almost touching about the way they were groping toward a new world. Although they shared no thoughtful political critique of their society and were rarely given to serious thought, they could hardly be dismissed as irrelevant. For in their own way, they were every bit as rebellious and subversive to the geist of the old Chinese Communist party as their dissident compatriots, who were being jailed for writing wall posters and underground magazines. Wang was not propelled by idealism or a belief in "science and democracy," nor did he appear to be particularly fascinated with power and wealth. He and his cohorts were lured onward by a vague and romantic thirst for a life which was more exciting and colorful, a life which they imagined to be possible in the West.

They were trying to construct a crude replication of the West from the little they knew about it, drawn to this apparent spot of brightness on their horizon. Like blind people, they stumbled along, some with virtually no real education, trying to append the symbols of this foreign fantasy world—clothes, music, cigarettes—onto their own lives, as if these few props might somehow elevate them out of the dullness of their own existence.

"Why is our life so boring when Western life is so rich?" one young woman asked me in the Peace Café, confessing that she was transfixed by what she had seen on Chinese TV when Deng Xiaoping visited the United States.

Washington. D.C.

In a small, windowless control room in the basement of NBC's Washington affiliate WRC-TV, thirty-seven coloı screens flicker just below a dozen wall clocks which show the times in various cities around the world. (Although there is still a "Saigon" clock, there is none yet for Peking.) On screen, two demure young models discuss a new disposable douche beside Ed McMahon testifying for a can of dog food next to a sky that suddenly fills with hundreds of dollar bills obediently landing in neat stacks. Katharine Hepburn flashes into existence, bicycling through the Welsh countryside, just as Richard Burton and Elizabeth Taylor are performing a raging version of *The Taming of the Shrew*. In the midst of this blazing collage, a Chinese face appears and begins to speak in Mandarin. It is Zhao Zhongxiang, the Central Television of Peking's network anchorman who is beginning his nightly broadcast feed to China on Deng Xiaoping's historic visit to the U.S.

Until this moment Zhao Zhongxiang, already dubbed "China's Walter Cronkite" by the employees of WRC-TV, has been pacing up and down the halls of the station intently studying tonight's script. Although contrasts between Zhao and his American counterparts are irresistible, they are hardly apt. Zhao is admittedly a well-known figure on Chinese television, but not the kind of media celebrity with which Washington is familiar. There are still no "communicastors" in China competing against one another in "happy talk news" for higher ratings. In fact, in China, with the exception of a few large cities, there is only one channel, and Zhao simply calls himself a news announcer. Nonetheless, Zhao created a minor stir among the American media people soon after he arrived in advance of Deng's entourage. First, he interviewed President Carter. Then, much to their surprise, they found him out on the West Lawn of the White

House underneath the arching elms taping a stand-up news-cast just as if he were one of them.

Now Zhao sits in Studio F at a stage desk normally oc-cupied by Tom Brokaw for Washington segments of the *Today* show. Except for the word "Today," which is covered over, nothing else on the set has been changed for the Chi-nese telecast. So Zhao's enthronement in Brokaw's chair and his temporary occupation of this borrowed TV environment suggest a man who has accidentally parachuted into someone else's private life.

Zhao begins his run-through with a film clip of Deng being welcomed on the South Lawn of the White House. The con-trol-room monitor on which he appears is almost surrounded by a kaleidoscope of American images, so that when Vice-Premier Deng flashes on the screen, it appears that he has momentarily forgotten the Chinese context from which he had just come.

What makes this pastiche of blinking televisions doubly confusing is the fact that at this very moment the Public Broadcasting System is also televising live the gala program being performed in Deng's honor at the John F. Kennedy Memorial Center for Performing Arts. Zhao winds down his brief introduction to the day's events on one screen, which shows Nixon arriving at the White House for a reception for the Chinese. Suddenly and incongruously the Harlem Globe-trotters materialize on the screen beside him and begin razzle-dazzling around the Kennedy Center stage; and just as the taped Deng Xiaoping flashes off the Peking broadcast, the PBS cameras pan up to another, assumedly realer Deng, who is sitting in a box at this very moment with President Carter applauding the pyrotechnics of the Globetrotters.

Watching this whole jarring collision of cultural images are two earphoned Chinese engineers. They sit stoically at the control console speaking by phone to Peking and readying for the final feed.

"What do you make of American TV?" I ask Ma Yushan, a sound technician sitting quietly in the viewing room behind the control booth.

She gazes blankly at the monitors. Closing her eyes, she smiles. "Very nice. Very nice," she finally says and then asks, "Who owns these stations?" wrinkling her brow in anticipation of a complicated answer.

I begin to flounder in Chinese as I try to explain American conglomerates. The only Chinese phrases my media-seared brain summons up so late at night are "bad capitalists" and "evil landlords."

"Have you watched much American TV since you arrived?" I ask, trying to rescue myself from the previous question.

"We've been very busy," she replies wearily. "We do turn the television on sometimes back in the hotel, but it's not always easy to tell where the programs end and the advertisements begin."

"Have you seen any of the American coverage of Vice-Premier Deng's trip?"

"Oh, yes. But they have so much," she says, laughing.

Indeed, the Chinese have become the object of one of America's most stupendous media spectaculars. Ratings for the Chinese coverage have been extraordinary. Even days before Deng's arrival, the anticipation of his coming filled Washington with such a sense of curiosity that it was unsated even by the avalanche of media attention which followed.

For weeks the press has been cluttered with background stories. The socially ambitious have vied for invitations to receptions honoring the Chinese. Businessmen (like their English forebears who, a century ago, fantasized unlimited possibilities for the mills of Lancashire if only "every China-man would add an inch to his shirttail") have been scrambling for contact with this promising new client. Even the insurance companies are charging into the breach. Besides their normal disaster coverage, they are now prepared to offer "political risk insurance" to China-bound corporations, lest the wheel of politics turn around once again and unleash a new army of Red Guards. Everyone, it seems, is enchanted with China's transformation; the unfriendly past is all but forgotten.

The task of making arrangements for the official Chinese delegation has been huge, but nothing like the headache of dealing with 950 members of the Western press accredited to cover Deng's visit. The media has descended on Washington like one of those flocks of migrating starlings that periodically sweeps down on some hapless town, blocking roads, covering the trees, and engendering cruel and unusual proposals for their dispatch.

At the Chinese Liaison Mission, officials completely surrendered before an onslaught of media inquiries. In the days preceding Deng's arrival, they did not even bother to answer the phone. As if Liaison Mission officials were not already sufficiently harried planning ceremonies and receptions, writing speeches and toasts, setting up tours and meetings, and arranging for security, a group of American Maoists from the Revolutionary Communist party (USA)—which still embraces the politics of the militant Gang of Four—showed up for what they billed as "a fitting welcome" for Deng Xiaoping. They hurled cans of white paint on the mission steps, fired lead fishing sinkers through the windows, and left an effigy, presumably of the "poisonous weed" himself, in the driveway.

In a press conference that followed at the Executive Motor Lodge, the RCP treated reporters to complementary Danish and coffee, while Central Committee Chairman Robert Avakian denounced Deng as "counterrevolutionary, a posturing bootlicker, and a sawed-off pimp." In the White House Press Room, more important controversies raged. What, for instance, was Deng's actual height? Different sources placed him anywhere between four foot eleven and five foot two.

At Blair House, where Deng was to stay, several freshly polished brass spittoons were carefully installed to accommodate the vice-premier's legendary habit of voiding his rheum while deliberating on matters of state.

Meanwhile, back in China, Deng's people were beginning to learn about America and getting ready to enjoy an unprecedented four-day holiday celebrating both the lunar new year and their leader's historic visit to the U.S. The Chinese press uncharacteristically called for "festivities continuing days without end with merry-making and recreation . . . so that people will have a good rest before plunging into work for modernization." As a special bonus, the masses were to be treated to a week-long U.S film festival, the first in three decades, featuring Charlie Chaplin's *Modern Times, Future World, The Hunchback of Notre Dame,* and a truckers' film called *Convoy.* (Now that the Chinese leadership has at last decided on the acceptability of showing foreign films, it is striking that the ones chosen seem to have been grabbed practically at random off the shelves of Hollywood distributors.)

In China and America, the stage had been set. On Sunday, January 28, 1979, a Boeing 707 with the characters for "China People's Airline" inscribed on the fuselage, glides slowly out of the gray winter sky onto a runway at Andrews Air Force Base. The pomp and ceremony of this impending moment makes it easy to forget that although Deng Xiaoping is coming from the world's most populous country, he is also from one of the world's underdeveloped countries. Despite the hundreds of American dignitaries and innumerable press here to welcome Deng as if China were a new superpower, a significant inequality between the host and visitor nation remains. Deng's arrival in an American-made plane barely suggests its magnitude.

The 707 reverses its engines with a roar and taxis into the apron. The hatch swings open. Suddenly, Deng appears in the darkened doorway like a cuckoo bird emerging from a wall clock to toll the hour. He pauses, smiles, and returns the applause of the well-wishers below. Then securely grasping the handrail, he works his way toward the crowd at the bottom of the stairs and is finally engulfed in a reception line of American officials who tower over him. When he reemerges, two pretty Chinese women present his cheerful wife, Zho Lin, and himself with bouquets of flowers tied with pink ribbons.

Both Deng and his wife step into a waiting limousine, and, almost as quickly as they have appeared, vanish. The occasion has been startlingly brief, but like a well-directed stage play, every detail has been executed with precision and duly recorded by scores of TV cameras. As Deng speeds away toward a rendezvous with President Carter, only one unruly detail remains. The chilly winter wind blows a lone pink bow across the Tarmac. A Secret Service agent, gripping the leash of a shivering police dog, dashes after it and finally subdues it with a heavy boot.

Before he even arrived, Deng Xiaoping had already succeeded in mesmerizing America. Not since Nikita Khrushchev barnstormed across the country in 1956 has a foreign leader attracted so much attention. After his first day in Washington, there is hardly a family in America who has not come to recognize Deng. Yet despite the vast exposure he is receiving, Deng does not really open up. He refuses all interviews, with the exception of one audience he grants television network anchormen. He refuses to hold any press conferences at which he could be questioned, even though the print media complains loudly. Although his face becomes familiar, his cool public demeanor provides few clues to his inner thoughts or feelings.

Buttoned up to his chin in a gray tunic, often seated so that his feet do not even reach the floor, this puckish man, whose right eye opens wider than his left, reminds me somehow of an Indian papoose. His smallness and his almost endearing way of cocking his head to one side and pursing his lips together when listening make it difficult to remember that Deng is a man of power and guile. As one looks at him, it is impossible to imagine that while he goes through his paces before us, he is actually planning an invasion of Vietnam. The fact that he speaks no English and makes only rare gestures to ingratiate himself with the Americans who swarm around him, lends him an even greater aura of fascination.

Actually, very little is known of Deng's life, a void which neither he nor his aides have made any effort to fill. Those few facts which are public have been circulating for days in the press, as if simple repetition might finally reveal his true persona.

Deng, born in Sichuan Province in 1904, traveled to France in the 1920s (although he professes to have forgotten all his French), where he met other Chinese leftists and joined the Chinese Communist party. He also went to the USSR for a short stay in 1926. We know that Deng was a veteran of the Long March, that in the 1930s and 1940s he served in the People's Liberation Army as chief of staff, and that he moved to Peking to join the Politburo in 1952 at the start of the Cultural Revolution. In 1966 Deng, then secretary general of the Chinese Communist party, was cashiered, labeled a "renegade, scab, and traitor," and paraded through the streets of Peking wearing a dunce's hat. He was then forced to write a humiliating self-confession extolling the thoughts of Chairman Mao and admitting to his own dereliction as a revolutionary. Even today, this long-winded document is painful to read.

His brother was reputedly hounded to suicide, and one of his daughters was crippled by Red Guard beatings. It would be surprising if he did not have some ambivalent feelings about Chairman Mao.

Deng made a comeback in 1973 and was reappointed vice-premier of the State Council. But with the death of his mentor and protector Zhou Enlai in 1976, Deng again came under criticism and "fell from the stage," as the Chinese say —only to emerge again in July 1977. With the fall of the Gang of Four, he was restored to all his previous posts.

It was an unusual second comeback in China, where until recently leaders were more easily defrocked than rehabilitated. His return to power not only signaled the end of the Gang of Four, but gave further impetus to the Sino-American rapprochement, which is now reaching a crescendo with his trip to America.

The Chinese seem to realize that their unprecedented journey to the U.S. means they are entering the age of high tech. Not only have they come here to establish an accord with the U.S. but to show their people back home what "modernization" is all about. As a result, they are paying scrupulous attention to every public detail of their sojourn as the first televised reflections of America are beamed back to China.

"The Chinese have been extremely appreciative of all the help they've received," says Ray Lockhart, one of several American producers in the WRC-TV studios who have been assigned by the three networks to follow the Chinese around the country, help shoot their news footage, and aid with the technical aspects of their nightly broadcast feed to Peking.

"They're not paying us anything. But they want to learn. It's just a good-will thing." He winks. "Of course, all the nets want to get their own people into China, and I guess this can't hurt."

"The Chinese are just like kids in a candy store," adds an engineer watching Zhao on a monitor. "Many of them have had very little experience with our fancy equipment. They must really be getting their minds blown. But they've read so much literature at least they know which buttons to push. They don't do much fancy shooting or editing. They love long, slow shots. They'll just start a camera grinding and show a whole scene or speech from start to finish.

"And then they adore good shots of American scenery. It's kind of an early fifties production. Nothing complex. But we've had no trouble from them, except they keep wanting to change stuff right in the middle of rehearsal. They really don't quite grasp the complexity of it all."

In the WRC control room, the multi-screened extravaganza continues unabated. On one monitor, Deng is now making his welcome speech from the White House as part of Zhao's news show. The volume for all the other programs has been turned off, so that the room is filled with Deng's voice alone, though the other screens continue to blaze with silent images. As Deng speaks, Perry Mason, a fundamentalist preacher, and Bill Cosby (substituting for Johnny Carson) also appear to be speaking Chinese with a Sichuan accent.

I glance over at Ma Yushan. She is not looking at her vice-premier as he extols the restoration of Sino-American relations. Her eyes are riveted on a screen high up on the top row of the bank of monitors. A shiny car careens out of control, chased by three police cars, sirens presumably blaring.

She turns and catches me watching her. As if trapped in an illicit act, she half laughs and half giggles with embarrassment. Our eyes meet, and we are both silent for a moment. Then she sits up and says, "There is so much we can learn from America."

It is January 31, 1979, and the sun has not yet risen over Washington, D.C., as our caravan begins boarding four 707's for the flight to Atlanta, Georgia.

On our press plane, there is a special section blocked off in the forward area for the thirty-three members of the Chinese press, which comprises their TV crew, a documentary film team, and print reporters from the *People's Daily* and the

New China News Agency. Their seating area is easily distinguishable from the back of the plane by the dense cloud of cigarette smoke which envelops it soon after take-off.

Although the Chinese press are identified with the same green and white dog tags (which erroneously read VISIT OF THE PRESIDENT) as the rest of us, there has been very little mixing. Despite attempts by various American and European writers to engage our Chinese colleagues in conversation, nothing much has happened. Since the Chinese tend to move in tightly knit groups, it is often difficult to know how to establish initial contact without appearing to be pushy or impolite.

As I wander forward into the haze to search for a State Department press aide, I suddenly feel someone tugging on my sleeve. Turning around, I find a New China News Agency journalist, whom I met briefly the other day at the White House, beckoning me to sit down in the empty seat beside him. As I seat myself, he unfurls a Washington paper and points to an article describing the aloofness of the Chinese press.

"Do you think this is true?" he asks point blank. I tell him that most American print reporters have, in fact, found their Chinese counterparts exasperatingly elusive.

He reflects for a moment and switches from English to Chinese. "I think there is a problem. In China, you know, things are still quite formal. We don't make acquaintances, particularly with foreigners, quite as casually as you do. Besides, since we arrived, most of us have been so overwhelmed just keeping up with our work that we've hardly had time for anything else. And then there is the language problem. That makes many of us quite timid. During the Gang of Four, *everyone* learned how to be timid."

He glances back at the newspaper article, which he has heavily underlined with a ballpoint pen.

"Anyway, things are better now . . . don't you think so?"

he continues, appending a question mark to what started out as a statement. "For so long, we have not had the opportunity to know foreigners. Really, it has been . . ." He does not finish the sentence.

Like so many Chinese, this friendly, earnest man, who later asks that I do not quote him by name, has never been abroad before. His English, which he speaks well although not idiomatically, has all been laboriously self-taught in China.

"How do you gauge the Chinese reception in America?"

"Why did Carter recognize China when he did?"

"Why are Americans so fascinated with China?"

These and other questions come in a burst. Suddenly, he stops himself as if he has passed over an invisible line and is taken aback by his own expressions of curiosity.

So I ask, "Do you think China's importation of so much Western technology will have any undesirable side effects?"

"Yes. Personally, I do have some apprehensions," he replies, lowering his voice. (It is the first time I have ever heard a Chinese use the word "personally" in discussing national issues.) "Let's just say I know what you mean by your question," he adds, showing no eagerness to pursue this line of inquiry.

"Are any high-ranking leaders concerned with this problem?"

"No. Not yet." He inhales about half an inch worth of smoke in one drag on a cigarette.

"When do you think they'll get concerned?"

"It is still early. Too much is happening now. Things are going so fast that there really has been no appropriate moment to reevaluate. But personally, I hope that we can modernize by taking only what we need from the advanced country and avoiding many of the problems with which you are already familiar. Anyway, that is my hope."

"Do you expect the new liberal Deng Xiaoping line to survive?"

"Well . . ." He sighs as if to indirectly acknowledge China's perplexing wake of deposed leaders and reversed political lines. "These things are hard to explain to a foreigner. We must wait and see. But I hope so."

Shanghai

The strings of Christmas-tree-like lights strung up and down the main thoroughfares of Shanghai have just blinked out. It is 10 P.M. The first evening of a three-day holiday celebrating the thirtieth anniversary of the founding of the People's Republic of China is drawing to a close.

The huge crowds of people who only an hour ago filled the streets of Shanghai to overflowing have now disappeared. People's Square, a vast parade ground in the center of the city reclaimed from an old English horse-racing track after liberation, is now almost empty.

This year, unlike so many past years when politics were "in command," there will be no fanfare or parades here at People's Square to celebrate China's Communist anniversary. The only suggestion of those tumultuous days of Maoist adoration is the massive portrait of the departed chairman that hangs behind the reviewing stand next to a likeness of his replacement, Hua Guofeng. In back of this oversized icon, the dark bleachers of the old race track still rise, evoking an ambience of times past.

A motorcycle and sidecar bearing two white-uniformed agents from the Public Security Bureau cruises down the parade grounds.

There is an autumnal coolness in the night air. I walk alone, savoring the solitude and openness of the square, having spent the day amidst endless crowds of people walking along the Bund, once the center of foreign commerce in China.

I sit down to rest under one of the ornate lampposts which dot the square, when off in the distance I hear a buzzing that sounds like several amplified mosquitoes.

I get up, curious to see what nocturnal phenomenon is making this noise, and spot three figures on mopeds hurtling down the far side of the square, running a slalom course among the lampposts. When the riders reach the far end of the parade grounds, they loop back and begin to weave in and out of the row of lampposts in which I am standing.

I watch them as they navigate their way toward me at full throttle, hunkered down over the handlebars of their mopeds like apprentice Hell's Angels.

The first youth to reach my particular lamppost wears wrap-around sunglasses, despite the darkness. It is not until he has almost passed me that he takes a quick glance in my direction, smiles, and waves. Then, before he reaches the next lamppost, his rear brake light blinks on. He stops and circles back. As he pulls up in front of me, he looks around to see if the coast is clear, then comes to a stop.

"Hey, foreign friend!" he says, hailing me with a broad, friendly smile. "Would you like to have a ride?" He gestures toward the purring moped.

"Sure."

He dismounts. I get on. After a moment of instruction, I twist the throttle back on this toy-sized Chinese chopper and aim myself toward Chairman Mao's portrait across the square.

The two-stroke engine rattles and pops as I gain speed. The cool night air sweeps back my hair. I have a sensation of immense freedom on the 90 c.c. machine in the middle of the expansive square—of being able to turn in any direction at any time without obstruction—a feeling that is enjoyable precisely because it seems so incongruous here in China.

I pass one lone couple walking and holding hands. They do a cartoon double take as I rifle by: a foreign devil, hell-bent-for-leather in the middle of Shanghai.

"Not bad, not bad," my congenial host says as I glide back toward the lamppost where he has been waiting. I dismount. He receives his bike back with obvious affection.

The name of my new-found friend is Shen Yongzhang. He is a tall, good-looking youth in his early twenties. He sports a neatly trimmed Clark Gable moustache, a tight-fitting cashmere shirt, which is unbuttoned halfway down his chest, and skin-tight, baby-blue bell-bottom trousers.

"Are you a student?" he asks.

"No. I'm a writer."

"Where are you from?" He kills the engine of his moped.

"The United States."

"Oh. Wonderful! Where do you think my trousers come from?"

He smiles proudly as I lean down to examine his bell-bottoms.

"Look. Look here," he adds before I can respond. He fumbles at one of his back patch-pockets until he locates a small label sewn into the seam. It appears to say LEVIS.

"Do you see that? Now tell me. Where do you think these pants come from?"

"Well, it looks like they must come from the U.S.," I reply obligingly.

"No! No! Wrong!" He surprises me with the vehemence of his denial. Then shifting his weight from one hip to the other over his bike, he says triumphantly, "I made them myself, including the label. I made a pattern of some pants that an overseas Chinese friend had, cut out the cloth, and sewed them up myself."

He gets off his bike. Kicks down the stand. Does a complete turn-around with elbows slightly raised as if he were fashion modeling a new line of sports clothes.

"Not bad, huh?" He is grinning from ear to ear.

Examining Shen Yongzhang's pants more carefully, I can see that although convincing from a distance, they are indeed homemade. Not only is the machine stitching wavy, but in one place the inseam is coming unsewn. Nor is the LEVIS label an original but a replication done with a ballpoint pen on white cotton tape.

Unlike most Chinese youths who wear their hair in practical crew cuts, Shen wears his hair smartly trimmed, pomaded, and swept back in a fashionable wave so that tonsorially, he looks as if he might have come out a commercial filmed in Hong Kong or Singapore.

Of course, Shen does not know the West firsthand. His imitations are constructed on the basis of limited information. He is like a man enclosed in an isolated room trying to sketch the full dimensions of the outside world according to what he can see through the keyhole. Given such incomplete knowledge, the authenticity of his disguise is, in fact, no small triumph. Through sheer dedication and enthusiasm, he has somehow managed to create this enclave of Western affectation in the middle of China.

He remounts his moped and rests his elbows on its diminutive handlebars in a way which is at once cavalier and winsome: although he is a handsome young man who has mastered coolness, he nonetheless seems to be a gentle and pleasant person at heart.

What is disorienting about Shen is that despite his look of cultivated aloofness, he exhibits none of the negativism or sullen sarcasm that one usually associates with his pose and style of dress in the West. His friendly exuberance and openness are completely at odds with the image his clothes create.

"How much would a motorbike like mine cost in America?" he asks, taking a scrap of rag out from under the seat and buffing the shiny black gas tank.

"It's quite difficult to make a comparison."

"Well, how many years' wages would it cost?" he persists.

"Probably less than a month's wages for an average worker."

Shen pauses to digest the import of what I have said. Finally, he says almost reverentially, "I saved five years for this one. It's made in Jinan, Shandong Province. This one cost me six hundred and eighty yuan [about $450]. I saved since I graduated from middle school. Now I work for the city at a power plant on the night shift. But since this is holiday, I have a few nights off."

Three more motorcycles and sidecars filled with Public Security police officers ride into the square and head toward us. Shen stops talking and without turning his head follows their progress out of the corner of his eye.

"It's OK," he says, lowering his voice. But not until after they have traversed the square and turned out on Tibet Road does he continue.

"It's OK. We're just making friends, aren't we? Our two countries are friends now, right? So why shouldn't we talk?" he asks rhetorically, as if he himself needed assurance that our conversation was not still considered a nefarious activity.

"Do the agents from the Public Security Bureau mind if you're out here on your bikes racing around at night?" I ask.

"Oh, it's all right," replies Shen diffidently. "But we wouldn't have dared do it during the Gang of Four. It was considered really bourgeois. They would have hounded us and criticized us for not being home studying politics."

"What about now?"

"Well," he begins, just as one of his confreres peels up and stops beside us with a skid. "We can do what we want now. Getting rid of the Gang of Four was like a second liberation for us."

Shen turns to his friend, Li Baomin, and introduces him to me. He is also wearing dark glasses, bell-bottom pants, and a tailored cotton shirt.

Again, several Public Security Bureau motorcycles turn into People's Square.

"They're just cruising," says Li. "Here, let's walk over toward the reviewing stand. If you're not walking they think you're up to no good."

Both youths get off their mopeds and begin to push them by the handlebars. We start walking across the square as the motorcycles bear down on us.

"If they should stop, just speak Chinese and they'll think you're a student," says Shen. "They don't bother foreign students. Don't tell them you are a writer." Then, taking a comb out of his pocket, he gives his pomaded hair a few artful licks and pats it as if to make sure he is properly groomed should a confrontation arise.

"Just look in the other direction," says Li through the side of his mouth. "That way they won't be able to see that you're a foreigner."

I turn my head. The motorcycles glide by.

"Do you have much opportunity to talk with foreigners?"

"Not really," answers Shen dispiritedly. "We'd like to. There are a lot of young people now who just go up to foreigners on the Bund. They want to practice English. Everyone wants to speak English. But, unfortunately, we don't know how." He looks with resignation at Li. "When we were in middle school there were no classes in English, so we never learned."

The admission that he cannot speak any English seems to depress Shen. Indeed, it is ironic that these two youths, whose appearance suggests such accomplishment in the pursuit of foreign styles, cannot speak the language of the world they seek to imitate. Nor does it seem likely that, as power plant workers, Shen and his friend will ever learn. It is the fatal flaw in their efforts to transform themselves. Like actors, they are eternally fated to play characters they can never become.

Suddenly the floodlights which have been bathing the visages of Chairman Mao and Hua in bright light blink off. It is after midnight. Besides the other two mopeds which continue their frenzied buzzing around People's Square, there is virtually no one else out.

Shen offers Li and me cigarettes. I refuse politely.

"Hey! What about American cigarettes?" he asks, regaining some of his early joviality. "What about Loto Pai [Camels] and Luji Pai [Lucky Strike]?"

"And what about American cars?" asks Li. "Do you have a Fu-te [Ford] or a Da-zhe [Dodge]?"

Both youths ask their questions not to elicit answers but to display proudly their knowledge of such forbidden foreign goods.

"Did you know that the government now allows Chinese people to buy foreign cars and import them?" asks Shen. "All that you need is the foreign currency. I heard of one person who got it from a relative in Hong Kong. But so far I don't think there are more than a few people who have them."

"Does everyone own a car in America?" queries Li.

"Yes. In fact, some people have two."

Again our conversation is interrupted as several more Public Security Bureau motorcycles pull into the square. They pause and watch the other mopeds speeding around at the far end.

"They're patrolling again," advises Li. He looks over at the notebook in which I am writing.

"It would be better to put that away. If they come by and see someone talking to us and writing things down, they'll probably think you're a spy. There are still a lot of spies running around."

"But Li and I both feel very friendly to foreigners," Shen hastens to add, lest I take umbrage at even the merest suggestion that I am a spy. "I'm not sure why they always talk so much about spies. I mean, who are these spies? You're not Russian. You're an American." He laughs.

"Sometimes," adds Li, "I think that all those cadres are a little too much. They can't even tell the difference between a foreigner and a spy, but if they catch you talking with a foreigner, they start rumors about you."

"Does everyone in the United States have cassette tape

recorders?" asks Shen, shifting the conversation back to concrete affairs.

"Most anyone who wishes to have one can afford it, but since radio stations play popular music all day long, most people don't bother with them."

"Do you like disco music?" Before I can answer, Shen adds, "We're very fond of it. Sometimes we can get cassettes with disco music from overseas Chinese who visit Shanghai."

"Do you like to dance then?"

"Of course," responds Shen brightly. "But the government won't allow it in public any more. They closed down the only dance hall in Shanghai last spring. Now there is no place to go except our own homes, which are so cramped."

"I suppose you go dancing every night in the United States," Li says somewhat enviously.

"One can. But most people don't," I explain, trying to be truthful without utterly deflating the expectations of these two Western enthusiasts about the El Dorado from which I come.

"Do your friends like to drink a lot?" asks Shen as we finally reach the reviewing stand at the side of the square.

"Some do. How about young people here in Shanghai? Do they like to drink a lot?"

"No. Oh, no," say Shen and Li almost in unison. "Young people don't drink much in China. But we love to smoke cigarettes." With satisfaction, Shen exhales a large cloud of smoke into the night air. He again offers me a Double Happiness cigarette which, since I do not smoke, I refuse.

"Hey! Don't be so polite!" he protests. "If we're going to be friends, you can't be so polite," and again offers the cigarettes, which I decline as tactfully as I can.

The last lights on the ornate lampposts, which have been serving as the slalom course, blink off. It is after one in the morning.

Seeing no further signs of Public Security Bureau motorcycles, I take out my notebook to exchange addresses with Li and Shen. As I write, both of them admire my American-made felt-tip pen. I ask if they would like to have it.

"No. No. We don't want it," they quickly protest, making me suddenly feel like a GI trying to dispense gum and nylons to the ravaged natives.

Neither youth, however, has the slightest compunction about giving his address.

"If you have time, come and see us. Anytime," says Shen, a cigarette rakishly drooping from his mouth as he kick-starts his moped.

"OK. We'll be going." Li smiles and gives a quick wave. Then both youths open their throttles with a decisive twist and buzz down the center of People's Square, past the dark-ened portraits of the two chairmen.

Atlanta

The Ford Assembly Plant in Hapville, Georgia, is a massive, graceless configuration of low-lying gray buildings that sprawls like a military base across one hundred and nineteen acres of suburban Atlanta. In the gloomy front lobby of the main building, Henry Ford II, tall, silver-haired, and distinguished, waits with a squadron of nervous lesser corporate luminaries. They chat, tinkle change in their pants pockets, and cast quick glances out toward the front parking lot.

Suddenly, a shiny Lincoln Continental glides up to the door and stops. The executives immediately form a straight line as if on review. Henry Ford II, grandson of the man who said, "History is bunk," stands at the head of the column, exercising his special executive prerogative by being slightly out of line. His guests, as inclined as his grandfather was to defy history, are now arriving, ready to explore another aspect of their former adversary's industrial might.

Solicitous Secret Service agents leap out of a second car in the motorcade and open the doors of the Lincoln Continental. Deng Xiaoping steps gingerly out and looks around. He is immediately squired through the front door toward his waiting hosts.

Ford smiles and, towering over his guest, greets Deng with an expansive handshake. Then he shepherds him down the receiving line, one hand gently cupping Deng's elbow, the other steering him from behind in a corporate quadrille.

With the greeting over, the entire troop, which includes U.S. Ambassador-Elect Leonard Woodcock and Chinese Minister of Culture Huang Zhen, each with his sundry retainers, heads down the corridor, through an open door, and into the roar of one of the plant workshops. In front of them is a fleet of chauffeur-driven golf carts. The entire ensemble boards this fleet of dodge 'em bumper cars like children at a midway, and quickly disappears behind racks of doors, hub caps, and fenders.

About thirty members of the press pool who have been hemmed in against a FoMoCo photo display by a security rope are released. Like hounds chasing a fox, they charge down the corridor after Deng. Their destination is what White House press officers have listed on the schedule as "First Photo-op," the first place where reporters will actually be able to see Deng and his entourage in the workshops. So unwieldy has the press corps become that only select "pool" reporters have been allowed to enter the plant; and having been excluded from the procession of golf carts, even they will only catch fleeting glimpses of the Chinese as they speed down the assembly line.

The sight of ten gold golf carts filled with Chinese Communists immediately distracts most of the Hapville Ford plant proletarians from their labors. "Hey, Chi-Coms," one worker bellows out. But the spectacle of fifty stampeding members of the press, weighted down by cameras and tape recorders, some daredevils even trying to take notes on pads as they run, reduces workers to complete disbelief.

Just before Deng pulls in, the press gallops breathlessly up to a spot on the assembly line where two men are dropping engine blocks onto chassis. Members of a Chinese documentary camera crew, who were initially quite timid, have now mastered the dog-eat-dog world of Western news gathering. Led by an aggressive middle-aged woman, they push so far in front of the others that one of their Western confreres begins screaming at them, "Get out of the way! You're ruining my shot!"

As the Chinese crew backs off, Deng's golf cart arrives. The moment he steps off it, all the TV lights snap on and flash bulbs begin popping, bathing him in a blinding glare.

Deng walks right up to the assembly line and watches with silent curiosity as hanging engine blocks move slowly forward on a ski-lift-like overhead track to converge with the car chassis. Plant manager H. R. George in his business suit stands next to Deng, in his Sun Yat-sen tunic, endeavoring to explain the complexities of this industrial process over the din of machines.

As I watch Deng standing here, dwarfed by the vast technological splendor of the Ford plant, my mind floods with images of China: roads blocked by slow-moving oxen and donkey carts; fields laboriously plowed by bullocks and water buffalo; city streets filled with bicycles as the Chinese "masses" go to work; and the large Shanghai factory in which I worked in 1975, where the workers still moved the electrical generators they built from bench to bench without the benefits of assembly-line automation.

Compared to the impersonal efficiency of the Hapville Assembly Plant, the Shanghai Electrical Machinery Factory seems almost quaint. In the hugeness of this American industrial complex, one into which whole trains can be driven, Deng appears all too mortal, while China's plans to "catch up" with the West by the year 2000 seem incredible, and probably impossible.

It is strange to confront such thoughts at a moment when the Chinese appear to be rushing hellbent backwards into that nineteenth-century era of "borrowing," when they first bought whole arsenals and naval fleets abroad and tried to reassemble them in China, with disastrous consequences. Deng, however, does not give any evidence of being intimidated by such considerations. He watches with absorption and equanimity as the 1980 LTDs are assembled before him for American consumers.

When Deng's lieutenants speak of their formula for developing their country, "The Four Modernizations"—industry, agriculture, science and technology, and national defense—it all sounds so simple: a neat, surgical procedure whereby the best features of the industrialized West will be introduced into

China like an organ transplant. But is anyone calculating the likelihood of tissue rejection? The possibility that the spirit which comes with Western technology may wreak unintended havoc on Chinese society?

The juggernaut of Deng's tour moves irrevocably onward. His last stop at the plant is the end of the assembly line, where cars roll off at a rate of almost one a minute, more than 200,000 units a year, a far cry from Chinese auto plants, which altogether produce only 13,000 units a year. Dismounting from his cart, Deng is steered by Ford executives toward a lone worker. He chats with him briefly through his interpreter. Then he turns, and for a moment stands with his arms behind his back, watching admiringly as one after another the new LTDs come to the end of the assembly line like plastic toys extruded from a pug mill. It looks so easy.

As a shiny, yellow, four-door sedan dolled up with imitation leather roof, wire wheels, automatic transmission, push-button windows, air conditioning, and an AM-FM radio rolls off the line, Deng takes several steps toward it, pauses, and finally pats it admiringly on its glossy hood.

After his 1974 visit to the United Nations, Deng had proclaimed, "America is full of tall buildings and big cars, all totally devoid of beauty." Now, on this journey, far from wishing to distance himself and his country from America and its industrial progeny, he wants to establish a more tangible connection. Benignly patting this American car as Chinese TV cameras roll, Deng is sending a clear signal to his people back home. In this one fleeting gesture, he seems to be announcing that it is again permissible to aspire toward such Western luxuries; that it is again proper to exalt technocrats who can turn out such sophisticated mechanical marvels, to speak English, and to look with unalloyed admiration at the industrial harvest of the West.

I watch Deng nodding approvingly as plant manager George shouts some final words of explanation into his ear, and I wonder what those westernized Chinese who suffered so for their affectation after 1949 think as they watch their leader back in China on their factory television sets. It would most assuredly seem like a cruel and ironic twist of fate to have the "verdict reversed" on their lives so long after they had been discarded as bourgeois "demons, freaks, and monsters."

Peking

Although the air is still warm, the leaves have started to fall. I walk down the quiet, orderly streets of Embassy Row trying to guess the nationality of each delegation by the propaganda photographs posted in glass-encased bulletin boards out front. Having failed on the embassies of Gabon, Ethiopia, and Finland, but hit the mark on the Embassy of the German Democratic Republic, I pause in front of one more display case. Curling photographs within show a beaming uniformed general shaking hands with Muslim peasants.

As I am pondering the nationality of these portraits, I sense the presence of someone behind me. I turn to find a young woman also inspecting the display.

"Can you read English?" she asks, breaking the silence.

"Yes."

"Oh, very good. Where do you come from?"

"The United States."

"Oh. Also very good," she exclaims with a smile, as if she were praising a student for a good recitation.

The delicate young woman by my side is Ling Mulan. Her sparkling energy and curiosity seem to overrule whatever inhibitions she might have about striking up conversations with people in the street.

"Are you a student?" she asks expectantly.

"No. A writer."

"Oh, I see." She pauses to consider this new piece of information.

Laughingly, I request equal time to inquire about her.

"Oh, yes. Please. Help yourself," she says confidently.

Mulan is twenty-six years old. She is a second-year student at Peking Normal College. Her father is an official. Her shiny black hair is plaited in two short braids which hang down onto the shoulders of her gray jacket. She wears loose-fitting navy-blue pants, sheer tan socks, and black pumps with low heels, attire which would hardly distinguish her from other young women her age here. It is her lovely face that stands out, almost as if it were disconnected from the rest of her rather drably clothed body.

What one notices about Mulan's face is that it radiates intelligence and alertness. She looks as if she were permanently on the verge of a reaction, just waiting to be provoked into a smile, a moment of puzzlement, or even a frown.

"I like to take a walk each day," she replies when I ask her where she is going.

"Shall we walk together awhile and talk?"

"Yes, if you please," she replies, switching from Chinese to her stiff English which contrasts oddly with her spontaneous manner. "Perhaps we could chat some in English. I would like that. Let's go to Ritan Park. It is so near."

After we depart from what turns out to be the Pakistan Embassy, I ask her if she will tell me about her past.

"Do you really want to know?" she asks, cocking her head to one side, not quite sure why a person whom she had just met would ask such a question.

"Yes," I reply. "I am very curious to know."

"Well . . . it was . . ." she begins to speak haltingly, trying to decide where to cut into the story of her life.

"Over the last fifteen years there have been very few people who have led normal lives, at least not in the cities. I myself got sent off to work for six years in central Mongolia when I was only fifteen. That was in 1969. Can you imagine that? I was just fifteen. Still a child." She speaks without pauses, as if having once started, she could not control the avalanche of thoughts and memories.

"My work camp didn't have a name. None of them did. All it had was a number. We didn't have any bricks, so we had to build our house out of mud. There were ten of us girls who all lived together in one room inside a small earthen shack with a thatched roof. But we were no different from thousands and thousands of other young people who got sent away to distant places in the countryside to work after middle school.

"Conditions were very poor and life was hard, particularly during the winter, when the weather turned cold.

"When I first arrived in Mongolia, I felt indescribably sad. As a little girl, I had never imagined that I could end up in such a wild place.

"Before we left, the People's Liberation Army soldiers came to our school and told us that the conditions in Mongolia were very wonderful. They said that we could ride horses every day and go out walking in the grasslands. They said that it was a nice place to live and that we would be allowed to come back home and visit our families every year.

"We were called Soldier Farmers. Our group was organized by the army into units with military names, although we did not wear army uniforms. We dressed just like the peasantry.

"After we arrived in Mongolia, we found out how different circumstances were from what we had been told. Certain times of the year there would be wild dust storms which would rage down onto the farm where we worked. They would engulf us for days at a time. How can I describe how raw and cold it got up there? In the bitter winter with no heat we were never able to take a bath. In our shack, our only light was one oil lamp for ten of us. There was no electricity at all.

"Every morning we would arise at six. Our leader would blow a whistle and we would all dress quickly, sometimes in fierce storms, and go outside to exercise before having our breakfast.

"The food was very poor. All that we had to eat was . . . well, during the summertime we ate almost nothing except potatoes. Really! That's all! Potatoes!

"During other times of the year, we ate what we called black wheat—corn and flour made out of some kind of sweet potato that we often used to bake bread.

"Even though the food was very tasteless and coarse, I ate a lot. We worked so hard that we had to eat a lot. I actually even gained a little weight." She laughs at this thought, since she is now quite slender. "But my body was strong and my face was brown just like a peasant's, from all the work outside.

"There was one group of people on our farm who were politically very active. They never complained about anything. Being so stalwart was considered very revolutionary. But it was hard to tell what these activists were really thinking, what was really in their hearts. When I felt depressed or sad, I would never admit it to them, even though they were supposed to be our leaders. I wouldn't tell a soul, except maybe my closest girlfriend. I would just hide it inside me."

Mulan is consumed by her memories, lost in her own narrative the way a musician can become lost in a score.

"When we found out that they would not allow us to return home after the first year—the one thing we looked forward to more than anything else—we were desolate. They told us that unless we were married, we would be allowed to go home only once every three years.

"I thought my heart would burst with loneliness. During the spring festival, I remember thinking of my family, and weeping."

She pauses as we cross the street to Ritan Park. I buy two tickets at a window by the main gate for three yuan each, and we walk inside.

"I always thought about home," she continues, smiling sadly. "Because I could never succeed in banishing those feelings from my heart, I felt a tremendous conflict. On the one hand, I wanted to answer the call of the government. On the other hand, I was homesick because the living conditions were so hard and I was just a young girl far away from home.

"No one really took care of us. They gave us a lot of political education. This would stir up our spirits a little, though not very much. But we had no experience in how to lead our own lives. No one gave us any counsel, any comfort or advice about growing up. And young girls like ourselves, who had just come of age, felt that need particularly strongly."

As we walk through the park, people stop to stare at the unusual sight of a foreign man and a Chinese woman to-gether.

"Our farm was very large, although it was a hundred and fifty kilometers away from the nearest town, a small town at that," continues Mulan. "We were part of a huge movement that saw thousands of young students sent right out of school to Mongolia to 'learn from the peasantry.' But actually, we didn't live with peasants and we rarely even worked with them. We were isolated, by ourselves. We were 'volunteers.' That's what they called us, although actually none of us had much choice. We went because they told us to.

"Of course, we had some happy times, too.

"We spent our days cultivating vegetables or potatoes or wheat," she continues, as if the substance of those "happy times" had somehow eluded her.

"Sometimes when there were no crops to tend, they would put us to work with carrying poles and baskets to repair roads.

"In the wintertime when the fields were frozen, they sent us up to a large lake in Inner Mongolia called Ulan Cu Hai. When the lake finally froze over, we went out onto the ice to cut down the tall reeds which had grown around the shore during the summer. The reeds were used to make paper and thatch for roofs, as well as a certain kind of mat which is woven by the peasants who live along the lake. Do you know the kind of reed mats we Chinese sleep on during the summertime to keep cool? Those peasants could weave all kinds of beautiful things.

"Each winter when we went to Ulan Cu Hai, we actually did live for a while with the peasants beside the lake. I think that the peasants up there in those remote areas, far away from the turmoil of the big cities, were quite happy. They fished, made mats, and went about their lives. But when our group of young people arrived, a lot of contradictions developed. I think we ended up having a very disturbing influence on the lives of those native people. The government not only controlled us, but they started trying to control the lake and the peasants around it, telling them where they could live and cut reeds, where and when they could fish, and generally bossing them around.

"Before we arrived, the peasants could do pretty much what they wanted to. It all began changing when we arrived. It wasn't long before their lives started to be in a turmoil."

Coming upon an empty and secluded park bench beneath a locust tree, we sit down.

"Perhaps from the long-range perspective, the whole policy of sending us up to Mongolia benefitted the country," sighs Mulan. "But if it did benefit our country, it is not so certain in my eyes whether or not it benefitted the peasants there, even though the cadres used to say that everything was done for them."

Several young boys who have been playing with homemade slingshots in the park spot us and wander over to watch our conversation. It is not long before other, older onlookers have also fastened themselves barnacle-like around the spot where we sit. They stand absolutely still and stare with such absorption and concentration that if one could not see the object of their curiosity, one might imagine they were watching daredevil feats on television. But no! Emboldened by each other's presence, they are simply looking at us, indulging in a benign voyeuristic phenomenon, something a foreigner soon gets used to in the public places of China.

Sometimes when thoughts pile up in her mind faster than she can speak, Mulan will break into Chinese. And so, even though she wants to seize the opportunity to speak English, our conversation alternates between English and Chinese. But not wishing to provide this armada of onlookers with a sound track, she now concentrates on speaking only English, a crowd-repelling tactic that we are to perfect in our subsequent meetings.

"Actually, I don't care if they look," she says finally, beginning her remark with what must be her favorite English word. "They have not had a chance to see a lot of foreigners, so they like to have a close-up look. You don't mind, do you?"

Indeed, I do not. I am lost in my own thoughts, marveling that I should at last be sitting in a public park in Peking with a young Chinese woman. By itself, the idea is, of course, hardly unusual. But in the context of China and its last thirty years of isolationism, my presence on this park bench beside Ling Mulan seems like an astonishing accomplishment. I cannot help but recall roaming these same streets and parks alone in past years without the remotest hope that any Chinese my own age of either sex would stop and engage me in conversation.

"At first, we had a lot of energy because we were young," says Mulan, returning to her Mongolian odyssey. "We were full of imagination and a sense of possibility. We thought that it was right that young people learn how to live under difficult conditions just as Chairman Mao had done when he was a youth. We felt that we had an obligation to try to reshape our world view through hard physical labor. We thought such work would help harden our spirit and resolve.

"I tried very hard to reconcile the contradictions between attending to my own life and serving my country. I wanted to meet the needs of the country and apply myself to its reconstruction. So I studied Chairman Mao diligently by that small oil lamp. Anyway, besides one elementary English text that I managed to bring with me, there was nothing else to read."

She clasps her hands in her lap and turns directly toward me. "You know, I still think about that contradiction, between the need to serve one's country and one's self. And I still don't know how to make the two harmonious.

"In Mongolia we had so little time for ourselves. Of course, boys and girls were separated on our farm. For the first few years, we never worked together or were not even allowed to see each other. Actually, we girls seldom thought about boys anyway, since we were much too young to marry.

"But finally, during that last year, after the army had left, discipline began to break down. Then we were able to meet with the boys. We began to see each other in the evenings, to cook meals for each other, and talk. Before that, we had all eaten in a large, cold, and dirty canteen.

"We were so starved for any kind of entertainment. We just wanted to laugh and be around people who cared about us.

"Of course, most of the girls on our farm eventually wanted to get married. But they didn't want to marry in Mongolia. They wanted to return to Peking first. They feared that if they married up there, they might never be allowed to move back home. And even though there were some girls who were getting past their late twenties—when it is customary for a young woman to become engaged in China— they could not allow themselves to think of such a thing. If you were a beautiful girl and living in Peking, you could, of course, make a very fine match with a man of good position. But in Mongolia, all you could find were ordinary workers.

"Even so, some girls did end up marrying in Mongolia. And they're still there now. But I think they are probably very sad. I mean, how could . . . ? You would always be homesick for your family and city. How could they forget such things?

"The only other alternative for a girl was to marry a boy whom her parents had picked out in Peking, a boy she had hardly even met. She might have a chance to get to know him when she went home for her short visit. But she would have to get married quickly before she left again. But then, of course, even though she had to separate right away, she could go back every year rather than every three years. So, some people finally got married that way."

For a few minutes, Mulan is immobilized by some unspoken thought.

"We were just young people trying to do what was correct," she says, finally breaking out of her trance. "We were like wounded children. No one would acknowledge our wounds, since it was politically incorrect to be wounded.

"The only thing that made me really happy in Mongolia was to think of the future, to dream that one day I would be able to return to Peking.

"But none of us believed we'd ever make it home again," she says, shaking her head. "And perhaps I would still be up there were it not for the fact that I finally got seriously ill. I had an operation, and the doctor said that it wouldn't be good for me to continue doing heavy physical labor. So he wrote me a certificate—a ticket to come home after six years.

"I believe our farm is still up there, although it's been a number of years since I left. Most of the other students have returned home now. You know, in the last few months, tens of thousands of students have been pouring back into the city from the countryside. Even though there aren't any jobs for them, they're glad to be back home.

"I know that we all experienced many hardships in Mongolia. Of course, we weren't the only ones. But actually, even though those were bitter years, when I think back on it, I know that the whole experience taught me a lot about how to be strong. That's just the way things seem to be: everything has two sides."

Twilight has begun to settle over the park. The cicadas have started to sing. Even our audience has departed for dinner.

"Here," she says, taking my pen and pad as we reach the park gate. "If you ever want to get in touch with me, you can call and ask for me. Although the phone is at the front gate of the compound where my family lives, someone will come and fetch me."

She writes down her phone number. She is just beginning to write her address when she stops and says almost severely, "Please don't come to my home yourself. It is better to call or write a letter the day before. It would just not . . . you see, people here in *hutongs* [back alleys] are still quite conservative and they love to gossip."

She finishes writing her address and hands it back.

Before I can say good-bye, she states without any indirection or hesitation, "I am free tonight."

"How about tomorrow?" I counter, ruing my dinner engagement with a friend.

"Yes. Please," she replies, pursing her lips as if to suppress a smile. "Where?"

"Across from the Peking Hotel on Wangfujing."

"Good." She smiles. "Good-bye," she adds with precision, and turns to walk away.

It is a fall morning bright with sunshine. I have waited almost ten minutes for Ling Mulan when I spot her running across the street just ahead of an impenetrable wall of moving bicycles. When she finally skips up on the sidewalk, she is breathless but smiling.

Today, Mulan's braids have given way to a ponytail which she has tied with a pink kerchief. She wears a new gray jacket with handsome brass buttons and a mottled black, red, and yellow blouse beneath. Other than these few attentions which she has expended on herself, her dress is the same as yesterday. And yet, like an exotic bird whose plumage undergoes subtle but colorful changes at the time of courtship, Mulan is in fact transformed. She has filled that small triangle that lies beneath her chin, and just between the lapels of her jacket, with color. She has fastened her hair, an area of women's fashion only recently liberated for cultivation, with a bright kerchief. She has focused her attention on those few details through which a respectable Chinese woman is allowed to express her sense of fashion.

Through a steady flow of sidewalk traffic we walk down Changan Boulevard toward the Gate of Heavenly Peace. Just across Tiananmen Square, the largest in the world, stands Mao's mausoleum, where the Great Helmsman himself lies stuffed beneath a crystal sarcophagus, testimony to modern taxidermy. Officials allow it to be open only three days a week now, as if limiting access to Mao's remains in death might somehow help put his life into more realistic proportions.

Today, the fervor of the chairman's politics seems more distant than ever before. Mulan and I turn away from Mao's tomb and walk through a gate in the crimson walls which surround the arching ochre-colored tiled roofs of the Imperial City.

"My father had a particularly hard time after the Cultural Revolution," says Mulan as we walk. "He was overthrown by political opponents and sent off to the countryside to work on a farm, just like I was. I didn't have any contact with him for years. Our family was scattered to the winds."

We find a vacant bench and sit down under ancient cypress trees, said to have been planted several centuries ago by the Ming emperors.

"During the time of my father's political trouble, I really

did believe that he was a 'capitalist roader.' That's what everyone was saying. What else could a young girl think? They claimed that he had hurt China. They said that he was a 'running dog' of this, that, and the other, and that I was ... I don't know how to translate it. But it means that since he was the 'running dog,' and I was his daughter, I was therefore something like a 'running puppy.'

"It took a long time. But later on I did finally come to appreciate that my father was not, in fact, a bad man but actually a good man who had been wronged. We never really spoke about it. We both just knew from what we had been through, something very dark and frightening, that we really did love each other after all."

It is quiet inside the high walls of this ancient imperial preserve. Honking horns from the street are barely audible. With the exception of two elderly men doing their morning *tai ji quan* exercises, the courtyard in which we sit is deserted. On this work day after a long three-day holiday, most people have returned to their jobs.

So accustomed does one become in China's cities to being surrounded by people, not only the throngs that stare at foreigners but also the endless flow of pedestrians and bicyclists on the sidewalks and streets, that it is an almost eerie sensation to find such relative solitude.

Like the sparrows that the citizens of Peking thoroughly expunged from the skies in the 1950s by beating gongs and drums so relentlessly that the frightened birds dared not land and, finally exhausted, fell to their deaths, two people in search of privacy in Peking rarely have any alternative but to keep in constant motion.

"Do you know how much I hate the Gang of Four for what they did?" This comment bursts from Mulan as if suddenly jarred loose by the thought of what happened to her father. "I think Chairman Mao's policy of suggesting that young people go to the countryside to live with and learn from the peasants was a good idea. But the Gang of Four wrongly used his policy. And there were a lot of officials supporting those who were not as good as they should have been. They weren't concerned with taking care of the people. They just wanted to make speeches and puff themselves up reciting a lot of slogans. It got to the point where they had slogans written on almost everything in China: on walls, dishes, trucks, luggage, towels, chimneys. They thought that you could make a country out of slogans. It's all right to say that we must work hard for the country to catch up with the modernized nations, but I don't like it when they say we have to 'work hard to realize communism.' That's just another cliché. 'Serve the People!' 'Serve the People!' They say it over and over again! It gets so tiring! I think a lot of the big cadres just keep mouthing slogans to distract people's attention from their own privileges."

Although political sloganeering reached a crescendo during the Gang of Four and has since been notably de-emphasized (lately signs cautioning people to be careful driving or crossing the street fill the old signposts once emblazoned with Maoist exhortations), the same cannot be said for privilege among officials. In fact, new Letters to the Editor columns, which have begun appearing in many daily papers, are filled with accusations against high-ranking Party members and military officers for using their influence to secure privileges to good schooling, the best apartments, and cars.

The Shanghai and Red Flag model cars of the elect are easily identifiable because their rear seats are usually completely shrouded from view by dark pleated curtains, which the Chinese politely call sun shades. Needless to say, even on rainy days these "sun shades" are drawn, lest the "masses" peer in from one of their stifling packed public busses and see a corpulent People's Liberation Army officer rushing his wife downtown to shop or ferrying his children to school.

"In class, our teachers still tell us that socialism is better than capitalism," continues Mulan. "Well, that's all right to say if you believe it, particularly now that we can ask them to explain it. But why is it better? If socialism is better than capitalism, why is the West so advanced while we are still so backward?

"Some of the explanations the teachers give make sense to me. But the truth is that I really don't know what to think because I haven't had a chance to make a comparison or even to study the subject in any depth. Sometime I am going to visit these foreign countries and see for myself. Yes, I'm going to do that. Of course, it is not possible now. But someday I will go abroad to study." She nods her head emphatically, and I have no doubt that someday Ling Mulan will be one of the chosen few.

"Actually," she begins anew, "twenty-six is quite old to start my studies. But I lost so much time in Mongolia. Then, after I returned, I had to go to work in a factory for four years. It was a costume factory here in Peking. Although I was able to live at home, we worked almost as hard as in Mongolia."

She pauses a moment, absentmindedly rolls her school workbook—which contains essays in English by Benjamin Franklin, Mark Twain, Edgar Allen Poe, and other notables —into a tight tube, and then lets it unwind like a spring.

"First, I worked as a farmer. Then I worked in a factory. Now I am a student." She shakes her head and laughs at the apparent absurdity. "But it wasn't easy, I can tell you that. In order to pass the examinations to get into Peking Normal College I had to study hard on my own every day while I worked at the factory. A lot of people in the factory were very cynical and sarcastic about my efforts to get into the college. I wanted to learn English. In their narrow-minded estimation, learning foreign languages was bad. They were still influenced by that kind of Gang-of-Four thought which views everything foreign as tainted and evil. Even though the

Gang of Four had been overthrown, those kinds of people still despise anything foreign. They fear foreign influence. They used to call that attitude revolutionary. Actually, I think it is conservatism masquerading as revolutionary politics.

"If I speak truthfully, I must say that over the past ten years I have come to dislike politics very much. It has become so petty, just another means for people to climb up and over one another. I can't really feel enthusiastic about working for some vague goal like 'communism' or 'world socialism.' For me, such goals seem too remote, and I'm a very practical person.

"I'm not sure I know what the purpose of our lives is. I think a lot of Chinese are confused now by all the changes. No one quite knows what the correct line is, or even if there is one. For some people, hard work is happiness. I like to work hard. But I also enjoy my leisure time. I think it's a natural desire to want to take it easy and just be happy sometimes. No one wants endless work and strain. Who would want to have nothing but that in life?

"If you ask me, I think we Chinese need less political education and more practical training that will help the ordinary person change his standard of living. If a political policy can't change bad conditions, then it's not a good policy even if it is supposed to be 'revolutionary.' Policies should be judged by their results, not their slogans."

We sit for a while and watch several elderly women who wear black aprons slowly sweep their way down the courtyard with straw brooms.

"Perhaps I will become an interpreter," says Mulan suddenly. Then, as if still arguing with her old tormentors at the costume factory, she adds, "If no one became an interpreter, how could China learn anything from foreign countries? How would we learn new technology and modernize?"

"Do you think that you might want to live abroad?"

"I know that conditions are much better in countries like your own than here in China," she replies somewhat defensively. "Most educated Chinese understand this, although they used to tell us that America was all strikes, riots, and inflation. I think that I would . . . perhaps one would get to a place like America and it would be so nice that. . . ." She falters for a minute. "Well, whether or not a person would want to stay or return home would depend completely on their personality.

"You know, in the past I think that some foreigners actually thought that Chinese people didn't have personalities, that we were all just like *jiaozi* [steamed dumplings]. All the same. I had a teacher who said that a lot of foreigners look on Chinese that way. But actually, we're just as different, one from the other, as you are."

Suddenly, from the wall behind our bench comes the loud crackling sound of electronic static. Then a voice barks out over the loudspeakers, which are spread out around the large courtyard. The noonday news echoes off the walls and around the graceful old temples and pavilions in the Imperial City. The silence is broken.

Our conversation stops.

"Aiya! What a headache!" says Mulan. "Let's leave!"

We walk through the gnarled cypress trees back out to our beat on the streets.

"Well, where shall we go today?" asks Mulan with a broad, adventurous smile when we next meet, early one morning.

It is still quite chilly, and I cannot help but think it would be nice to continue our conversation over a cup of hot coffee in the Peking Hotel.

"I do not want to go there," says Mulan bluntly. Perhaps she knows that all Chinese entering the hotel must first register and that there is a buzzer at the front door which is pressed if some unidentified Chinese, particularly a woman, is spotted entering the hotel with a foreigner—so that he or she can be intercepted. Whatever the reason, Mulan is adamant.

We head off down Nansuize Street, which runs alongside the Imperial City.

"Of course I want what is best for myself during my life," she begins, unprovoked. She seems already to have decided what she wants to talk about today. "I think that is only human nature, although while the Gang of Four was in power, they used to claim that there was no such thing as human nature. They said that people's nature was determined by their class. That meant that if you had come from the bourgeoisie, it was impossible to be a good person, since being bourgeois was bad. They said that if you wanted to have nice things for yourself, it not only showed poor political consciousness, but was also indicative of a bad class background.

"They also said that there could be no such thing as genius apart from class considerations. They claimed that even beauty had a class nature. The whole idea was ridiculous! I'm not sure I can tell you what beauty is. But whatever it is, I don't think it has a class nature." She says this defiantly.

We have reached Chaoyangmennei Street, which runs between the Forbidden City and Coal Hill, and was built by the Yonglo emperor during the Ming dynasty with earth excavated from the moats which surrounded his new palaces. We have been walking aimlessly, lost in conversation, when I glance at my watch and suddenly remember that I have an appointment for an interview at the Chinese Foreign Ministry in twenty minutes.

"Well, then, I will come with you," announces Mulan without any concern over whether such an offer might appear to be forward. "But I think I will wait across the street for you. Do you understand what I mean?"

Her meaning is clear. It is strange indeed to see Mulan,

who is otherwise so open and confident, inhibited by the uncertain political climate around her. In spite of "liberalization," there is still a fear in China, a fear that one morning everyone will awaken and once again find the political world standing on its head.

We board a bus together. Mulan flashes her bus pass. I pay five fen to the ticket seller who sits behind a small counter just inside the rear door, dispensing tickets from a leather coin bag. Since we cannot find seats together, Mulan sits across the aisle from me, next to a woman with bound feet who holds in her lap a shopping bag bulging with apples, leeks, and cabbage. Mulan fixes her gaze out the window. I wonder what dreams fill her head as the bus passes sidewalks filled with the peddlers, tinkers, and produce salesmen who have been reborn on the streets of China since the fall of the Gang of Four.

When I have finished my interview and we are again walking together, Mulan asks, "Do you think Chinese women are beautiful?"

"Yes," I reply, laughing at such a loaded question.

"In my view, one of the things which makes a woman beautiful is a sense of delicacy. I think there is real beauty in genteel and elegant manners. I think in order for a woman to be beautiful, she must be slender, and should act with grace and politeness. I can sense immediately whether a person is beautiful just by the way she walks."

Mulan is off on one of her discourses that has a momentum of its own.

"Actually, I don't think that a girl who is simple or tough, or who uses a lot of coarse language, could ever be considered beautiful. That would show a lack of refinement. Nice, smooth, white skin is beautiful, not skin burned brown by the sun the way mine was when I lived in Mongolia. I don't find large people beautiful. And I think slender hands and fingers on a woman are particularly lovely."

She turns her own hands over to examine them. The backs look rough and chapped.

"That's from working in Mongolia in the cold," she says matter-of-factly.

"I think it is human nature to appreciate a woman's figure if it is beautiful," she continues. "But fat people don't appeal to me. Thin people are just skin and bones with no shape at all, no beautiful lines."

We cross the street to a small corner park adjacent to the exhibit hall of the China Art Gallery. Spotting two empty seats on a bench, we sit down. One middle-aged male comrade who has been dozing peacefully in the warm sun at the other end of the bench awakens and, when he sees us, sits forward in his seat, preparing to flee as if he were a startled animal. But then, looking around and seeing no other vacant benches (many are completely occupied by sleeping figures stretched out their full length), he decides to stay. As we talk, he loses his fear of my foreign presence. Five minutes later his head nods back again, his eyes close, his mouth opens, and he begins to snore contentedly.

"Here in China, you seldom get a chance to see a nice female figure," says Mulan, speaking of the human body without any suggestion of sexuality. "I think that's a pity. That's one reason why foreign clothes appeal to me. Not those short skirts or tight shirts, but dresses that show some shape. I love the styles and colors of Western clothes. When I worked in the costume factory, I used to make things for myself and then try them on and look at myself in the big mirrors we had down there. Did I tell you that one of the things I would like to do someday is become a fashion designer?"

I cannot help smiling at this disclosure, marveling anew that I should be sitting here at all, talking with the likes of Mulan. I still feel furtive, almost criminal, about engaging in such familiar conversation with her, as if probing the intimate details of her aesthetics and life might somehow constitute a kind of espionage.

"You know this business of foreign fashions and styles is a difficult one for China," she begins to say, breaking into Chinese as she often does when an idea overwhelms her.

I reach out to touch her shoulder, to remind her to practice English, since outside of school, this is the only conversation she has ever had with a native English-speaking person. As I withdraw my hand, I find myself almost shocked by the spontaneity and naturalness of my gesture. Even though there are a large number of onlookers on other benches, she does not shrink back from this moment of physical contact. She simply smiles and begins once again in English.

"We Chinese have traditionally been cut off from outside influences. I think we often resist foreign ideas at first. But when foreign influences finally do make an impact, we don't seem to know where to stop. We don't seem to know how to balance. Suddenly some people want to get rid of everything Chinese and have everything foreign.

"You've seen all the girls who have started to curl their hair up tight at the hair salons. But I don't think they really know what beauty is. They're just imitating. They have not had a chance to develop a sense of beauty. They think that if they can look like foreign models, they will be beautiful. Now there are some girls who have started wearing foreign hats. I think they're quite ugly and inappropriate. But I still don't think that our government should forbid people to wear them. Instead, they should try to explain what beauty and good taste really are. They should help lead the people toward it.

"How can you blame the people? They have a natural desire to decorate themselves. But because they've been forbidden to do it for so many years, they've forgotten how. How can they raise their sense of what is artistic without experimenting? It's too simple just to criticize them and say, 'Don't run after all those Western styles and habits. They're no good!'

"China is just beginning to open up again to foreign art, music, literature, and fashion. We are just beginning to be able to look at our own traditional culture without being afraid that its feudal contents will harm us. You could say that we are a whole country of people just beginning to learn over again what beauty is."

She looks down for a moment.

"I think to learn about what is beautiful is as important as learning about politics. The last twenty years in China have been as if we were sleeping and trying not to notice what is beautiful. Sometimes it makes me feel sad when I think about it. So much time lost."

We have been talking for several hours. My plane for Canton, and then the U.S., is due to leave Peking Airport in a few hours, and I have not yet gathered up my things for departure.

Mulan and I abandon our bench and walk out toward the street.

"Perhaps you could send me some books on English literature," she says over the din of honking horns.

I nod, and we both fall silent, overwhelmed by how recklessly we have allowed our friendship to grow and how quickly it will all now end.

We walk down Wangfujing to the bus stop, which is crowded with people. I feel the moment of my departure arriving with an irrevocability that is frightening. I am not clear how one says good-bye to a young Chinese woman at a busy bus stop in Peking with hundreds of people watching.

Suddenly, I see my bus, Number 201, bearing down on the stop. I feel immobilized.

"Good-bye," Mulan says suddenly, breaking the paralysis. She stands before me, sweeping a long strand of black hair out of her eyes with the back of her hand. Then, she thrusts her hand forward. I pull out my hand, which is wedged deeply into one of my pants pockets, take hers, and shake it. It is the only conceivable gesture of farewell under the circumstances.

"Good-bye, Mulan." I feel the poignancy of all those classical Chinese poems about the sadness of friends parting.

"Will you write?" she asks with a suggestion of a smile. "Perhaps you can correct the English in my letters and send them back."

"Yes. Of course I will," I reply, releasing her hand.

As I board the bus, Mulan steps into the tide of blue- and gray-uniformed workers moving down the sidewalk.

Through the front windshield, I follow the pink kerchief with which she has tied her hair as she walks. It floats like a colorful blossom on the current of black heads which surge down the sidewalk.

For a moment, I lose sight of it, as if it had drifted behind a wave. Then it bobs up again for a last split second before finally vanishing.

Houston

When I step out of the elevator into the lobby of the Houston Shamrock Hotel, I see twenty gorgeous Dallas cowgirl-like hostesses in tight jeans, western hats and shirts, their faces impeccably made-up as if each were about to walk onto a movie set. In fact, they are waiting to accompany our entourage onto busses heading for a rodeo organized in Deng Xiaoping's honor.

"Well, hi there! Haryu?" asks Pat Arn, flashing a mouthful of gleaming white teeth and settling her lithe posterior onto the arm of the seat opposite me as the press bus pulls away from the hotel. "Y'all care for a nice cold Lone Star?"

After Americans and Chinese have been served cold beer, Pat turns back to me and says, "We're just here as Texas good-will ambassadors. We're real proud to have the Chinese with us. Who knows? We might even get into the newspapers."

"What made you want to come to this Chinese rodeo anyhow?"

She laughs and preens her hair. "Well, there was this guy arranging it, and it just seemed like a good way to spend Saturday night. Anyway, I love to do crazy things!"

"How do you feel about communism?"

"Communism?" She repeats the word as if it had no relation to our conversation. "Well, I don't care for communism, because they could take all that we have," she finally replies.

"Yes. It would be horrible," chimes in a cowgirl just across the aisle, carefully licking her glossy red lips.

"Well, what images come to mind when you think of China?"

"I think of a cold place with real harsh people," says Pat. "But I don't know if it's true or not."

"I think of a kind of poor place with too many people," replies her friend.

It is raining hard as twilight settles on our strange caravan hurtling down the straight, flat highway toward our rodeo rendezvous. Outside our bus, there is no one, nothing but the open Texas range. At last we see lights through the rain-streaked windows. The bus turns into a parking lot. A peeling sign announces: SIMONTON RODEO ROUND-UP, WHERE EAST MEETS WEST. The town of Simonton consists of a liquor store, a post office, a general store, and a pecan warehouse. Minutes later, Deng's limousine, which has delivered him punctually to so many formal receptions, pulls in and discharges its celebrated passenger onto the muddy parking lot.

> *Whiskey River take my mind*
> *Don't let her memory torture me*
> *Whiskey River don't run dry . . .*

The strains of a country and western band carry out to the dark, wet night from the rodeo arena, where it is light and warm, and gum-chewing Secret Service agents with blown-dry hair professionally clutch their walkie-talkies. They keep themselves distinctly apart from a group of Fort Bend County sheriffs, several of whom lean on bales of hay in the front entranceway and languidly probe their teeth with toothpicks.

An earlier busload of Chinese arrivals are trying on western hats presented by the Houston Chamber of Commerce. In Mao suits and cowboy hats, these Chinese visitors remind me of a child's game in which a piece of paper is folded three times, then given to three successive people to draw a head, body, and feet, and finally unfolded to reveal a conglomerate freak. Several Chinese, apparently keeping these treasured possessions for photographer friends who cannot snap pictures while wearing cumbersome headgear, have two or three hats on their heads, one on top of the other.

"Sure they're Communists," barks Joseph Jefferson Burris, a red-faced native who introduces himself with a "Commodore, Texas Navy" name card. "But what do you give a dog to vaccinate him against rabies? You give him a little rabies, don't you? I don't even think this guy Ping is a real Communist anyway."

Underneath the arena grandstands, long tables for serving a barbecue have been set up. The citizenry of Simonton, strung out behind the endless counter, ladle beans, fork-up spare ribs and sausage, and slap thick pieces of barbecued beef down next to pecan pies on paper plates nervously held by bewildered Chinese officials.

Even though they are notoriously skittish about large pieces of red meat, none of the Chinese protest these bleeding badges of Texan hospitality. They just pass on down the line to a gigantic vat of potato salad as if they had judged this whole event so far outside their normal course of experience that any refusal would be useless.

"Look at those guys go for that barbecue!" comments a man in western wear and cowboy boots, who stands by the main door and identifies himself only as "Wayne. I live here."

"Did you see those Coke cans with the Chinese symbols on 'em on the TV news?" asks another Texan dispensing soft drinks. "Well, sir, if each one of them Chinamen takes a drink of one of those Cokes, that's a lot of Coke! Do you get my drift?"

"Are you from China?" a heavy-set woman serving ribs inquires of a *People's Daily* reporter.

"I beg your pardon?" He cups a hand behind an ear to hear better over the music.

"Well, goddamn!" she rejoins, apparently satisfied that he is from China. "What'll they think up next? Welcome to Texas, Mister." She shakes her head and laughs.

After having my own plate heaped with food, I walk up into the grandstands and sit down beside my acquaintance from the New China News Agency, just as the band begins a new song.

I didn't know God made honky-tonk angels,
I might have known that you'd never make a wife . . .

"So loud," he says, gesturing toward the band and surrendering in his battle to conquer a barbecued rib with a plastic knife and fork. "Is that jazz?"

"No. It's country and western music," I reply and try to explain briefly its origins, floundering in an attempt to describe the logic of its thematic fixation on heartbreak and desire.

When "Honky-Tonk Angel" ends, the band slides right into "Rollin' in My Sweet Baby's Arms." Several of the cowgirl hostesses who are just behind us spontaneously begin to twist and writhe to the rhythm of the music while remaining seated on the bleachers.

Startled, my dinner partner turns, stops chewing, and watches their sit-down choreography. His gaze lingers on them as he tries to decide whether to admit yet one more cross-cultural intrusion into his overloaded cranium. Suddenly, one of the women gives him a friendly, sexy wink. A smile slowly spreads across his face.

"This indicates your world of diversity," he says and returns to his unfinished rib.

"You know, I like Louis Armstrong," pipes up a retiring fifty-year-old *People's Daily* journalist on my other side. He too has been watching the women. The remark is so unexpected it startles me, and, touched by his effort to bridge the gap, I turn to watch this shy man eating his dinner and beaming with satisfaction. Glancing down, I notice that he has a hand-held tape recorder beside him on the bleacher. Its RECORD button is depressed; its reel is turning. Instead of interviewing the American masses here at the rodeo, this socialist scribe is quietly recording the music.

The band breaks into a square dance, and the audience

begins whooping and hollering. The cowgirls pick up the beat. They appear momentarily ready to burst from their seats into the aisle.

"What kind of music is this?" asks the Louis Armstrong devotee, picking up his pad and pen now to jot down a few notes. But just as quickly he puts his pad down again, and with obvious pleasure joins the crowd, clapping in rhythm to the music.

"I never thought I'd be sitting in a place like this with such a hat on," jokes my other acquaintance as the band takes a break and an American photographer closes in on our little group to immortalize the two Chinese cowboys on film. "You know what we mean in Chinese by 'putting a hat on someone'—don't you? It means a person is severely criticized for being politically incorrect."

For these Chinese, perhaps nothing more startlingly illustrates the disjunction between this new "Western era" and the "reign of the Gang of Four" than this man's ability to joke about the wearing of political "hats." Whether he speaks from bitter experience, I do not inquire. But the difference between the duncelike hats, which many Chinese accused of "counterrevolutionary activity" were forced to wear while being paraded through the streets of China only a few years ago, and the ten-gallon hat now atop his head is vast indeed.

"Have you ever been to a rodeo before?" yells one of the photographers.

"No. I've never even heard of one," replies my acquaintance with disarming sweetness.

Pat and one of her companions, Joan, find us. The *People's Daily* correspondent stares transfixed at these two examples of American pulchritude. Noticing him inspecting her skin-tight jeans, Pat asks, "Do you wear jeans in China?"

"No! No! Not yet!" The *People's Daily* reporter waves off the idea, laughing.

"You don't have blue jeans? My Gawd!" She puts her hand to her mouth in semi-feigned amazement. Pat and Joan glance at each other and laugh knowingly.

My Chinese acquaintance hesitates, then says, "But it's not so bad there."

Pat suddenly grabs at his arm. "Oh, you're all so fine and wonderful! We truly welcome you here."

After this heart-felt gesture everyone pauses, momentarily stunned.

"She has gladness in her heart," the *People's Daily* writer finally says in Chinese. He gazes at her as a father might look into the eyes of his child.

"Are you married?" He addresses both girls at once.

"No," replies Joan, who has told me earlier that she is divorced.

"Do you still live with your parents?" asks the New China News Agency writer.

"Oh, no!" squeals Pat, wrinkling up her nose.

"Then where do you live?"

"By ourselves!"

"Oh, I see."

The two young Texan women smile with a mixture of friendliness and indulgence at the naïveté of their visitors.

"Let's go get some Pepsi," Pat then suggests to her friend.

"For sure."

"Well, good-bye, Mr. . . . What did you say your name was?" Pat asks the New China News Agency reporter.

"Wu. Mr. Wu." He gives only his last name to keep it simple.

"Yes. Well, Mr. Wu, it sure has been a pleasure talking with you," says Pat, becoming the diplomatic spokesperson for both women.

"Me, too." Mr. Wu smiles in wonderment as the girls rise and walk down the aisle in search of a soft drink.

There is something clumsy but touching about this encounter. For the first time in decades, Chinese like Mr. Wu seem ready to allow themselves to be drawn into the dizzyingly different world of America without rigid resistance.

Before Texas, the Chinese visitors and their American hosts have been traveling side by side without actually touching, like two parallel expeditions each removed from the other's field of gravity. Up until now the encounters between the sides have been largely of a formal, ceremonial nature. Chinese officials, reserved with foreigners under even the best of circumstances, have been reticent about sallying forth too brazenly into this new world of experience that surrounds them. Instead, they have sought the refuge of their own group and language.

Ironically, it has taken Texans, who have long prided themselves on their American chauvinism, to smash through the protocol of this trip and blast their way into the hearts and minds of their Chinese visitors.

I am not quite sure how Texans, in almost every respect polar opposites of the Chinese, induce their visitors to let their hair down, even a little. But I suspect that at the bottom of this triumph lies the simple fact that most Texans either do not know who the Chinese are, do not like them because they are Communists, or just do not care one way or the other. Instead of trying to ingratiate themselves like everyone else, they simply go about the task of being their normal boisterous and hospitable selves. Their attitude seems generally to be: If the Chinese want to join in, fine. If not, no matter; events will go on easily enough without them.

Ever since they arrived in the U.S., the Chinese have been besieged by Americans of almost every kind who seek to curry favor for one reason or another. Some aspire to build hotel chains in China; some dream of selling steel mills or oil-drilling equipment; some desire to establish a special relationship with the Chinese in hopes of garnering invitations to visit China; still others toady to the Chinese simply because of

their new and unasked for role as the center of social attention. On the other hand, with nothing to gain themselves, the
people of Simonton, Texas, are confronting the Chinese
without any designs at all.

Suddenly there is a ripple of applause. Deng himself enters
the stands as three horsewomen circle the arena displaying
the flags of the U.S., China, and the state of Texas. Surrounded by his aides, ministers, and interpreters, pumping
hands like a small-town pol, Deng works his way down the
aisle toward a bloc of empty seats. As he approaches the rail,
in front of a large sign that says: REST ROOMS & REFRESH-
MENTS, a young girl on horseback gallops up and presents him
with a ten-gallon hat of his own.

The whistling, cheering crowd watches with delight as
Deng theatrically dons his new hat. And in this one simple
gesture, Deng seems not only to end thirty years of acrimony
between China and America, but to give his own people permission to join him in imbibing American life and culture.

But in the gesture there is also an implicit suggestion of
surrender, an abrupt arresting of China's historic resistance
to the West. This one stark act seems to reverse the whole
momentum of China's long-standing struggle over who will
yield to whom. Deng's acceptance of this western hat is a tacit
admission of how far the Chinese now seem willing to lose
themselves in a world of Sino-American rapprochement.

It was not so long ago in the flow of human events that
Lord Macartney, sent by King George III to Peking to establish relations with the Imperial throne, refused to kowtow and
perform the "three kneelings and nine prostrations" before
the Qianlong emperor. The year was 1793. Now, a new
leader of the Chinese people arrives on American soil for the
first time in history and, stepping beyond that ancient sym-
bolic struggle, is willing to make his own genuflection in a
rodeo arena; a temple of the American way of life.

No sooner has Deng received his hat than he is presented

with a young Brahman bull, a gift from a local rancher. Before the crowd has even finished applauding, Deng disappears from sight, and the gate into the arena swings open again. This time it is Deng himself who comes galloping out in an old-fashioned horse-drawn stagecoach. He circles the ring waving through the open window like a beauty queen on a parade float.

The American TV crews work their cameras like airborne tail gunners under attack. "At last we got to this guy," rasps a gruff but triumphant soundman, a cigarette drooping from his mouth.

The crowd does not quiet down until Deng has returned to his seat. Beneath their cowboy hats, his entourage sits serenely on their benches as if posing for an official Western-style photo at the Wall Drugstore.

A voice booms over the PA system: "Guide us in the arena of life. . . . Help us, Lord, to live our lives in such a manner that when we take that last ride up there, You as our judge will tell us our entry fees are paid."

The entire audience rises for the cowboys' prayer and remains standing as the two national anthems crackle over the sound system. All the Texans remove their hats and clap them over their hearts to the first strains of "The Star-Spangled Banner." However, my acquaintance from the New China News Agency, either unfamiliar with this patriotic ritual or not recognizing the song, stands with his oversized cowboy hat still aloft, only his ears preventing it from falling completely over his eyes.

"And now, a fine young cowpoke from Chute Number One . . ." announces a voice with a Texas drawl.

"*Xian-zai, yi ge hao-di niu zai cong yi-hao men . . .*" echoes the Chinese translation, as a Brahman bull and rider barrel out of the chute, right in front of Deng's seat and go bucking and heaving across the arena to an accolade of cheers and rebel yells.

Shanghai

It is a warm fall day in Shanghai. I pause for a moment while walking along Soochow Creek to glance at the headlines of a newspaper that has been posted outside the Postal and Telegraph Building in a glass case for public reading. I start to skim an article about a speech that Vice-Premier Ye Jienying has just given in which he calls the Cultural Revolution a "catastrophe."

Standing several feet away from me is a man who appears to be in his sixties. He keeps glancing toward me. He wears a freshly laundered gray tunic and trousers, a gray workers' cap, and black cotton Chinese-style shoes.

Somewhat unsettled by being watched this way, I finally turn toward him.

"So I see that you can read Chinese characters," he says after a moment's hesitation, still facing the newspaper. He speaks in slow but almost perfect English.

Several other readers have already glanced up at us. He refocuses his attention on the newspaper, as if he now wished to abandon the conversation he had started.

"I can read some Chinese," I reply. "Where did you learn such good English?"

By now everyone in front of the newspaper case has stopped reading and is looking expectantly at me and this other man, curious to see what will develop. Sensing how ill at ease the situation is making him, I ask in English if he will join me for a walk.

At first he does not reply. Then, still without turning away from the newspaper, he says softly, "Fine," and without further comment begins walking toward the Sichuan Road Bridge over Soochow Creek.

He does not say anything until we are across the bridge and heading down the other side of the river.

Finally, almost inaudibly, he says, "I have not spoken English for thirty years." He smiles wistfully, his hands clasped behind his back and his head down. He then falls silent again as we walk down Sichuan Road past blocks of European-style buildings.

"There." He points up to a tall building in the distance. "That's where I worked before 1949. I was employed by an American company as an accountant and as a Chinese and English typist. But it's been a long time since I spoke English, so please excuse me if I speak incorrectly."

In fact, he does not speak incorrectly and has only the barest trace of an accent. But he does speak slowly, haltingly, as if he were recounting a half-remembered dream.

"No one knows that I speak English except my wife, and perhaps some overseers at the Public Security Bureau in my district, where they still keep a file on me."

"Do you feel comfortable walking and conversing with a foreigner in public?"

He looks at me directly for the first time. His face is pale and drawn, but there is a gentleness in his eyes.

"Never mind *them*," he says, calling up unnamed tormentors. "In the past I have lived in fear. But now most of my life is gone. I am nothing more than a worker anyway. My children are grown. So what does it matter?"

A white-jacketed officer from the Public Security Bureau passes us on the narrow sidewalk carrying a fish from the market on a rattan thong. He eyes us, perhaps still not entirely comfortable with the idea of foreigners and Chinese walking together in Shanghai, once the European capital of Asia.

"My name is Huang Baoren. My job is to repair houses," my companion begins after the officer has passed. He speaks resolutely now, apparently having decided that if he is going to talk at all, he is going to do so freely. "I get up every morning at five-thirty and work until dark. For eighteen years I have done this. I am paid only thirty-six yuan a month [about $22.00]. It is hardly enough to live on. But I must do it or starve. Mostly they use me to carry things, heavy things on construction sites. But now I am learning to become a carpenter." He smiles ironically. "My career is advancing in my old age."

The streets of Shanghai are swarming with people this holiday afternoon. Everybody is celebrating the thirtieth anniversary of the People's Republic of China. As we walk down the narrow sidewalk, it is sometimes difficult to stay abreast of one another in the current of pedestrian traffic from the other direction.

When we become separated, Huang walks on ahead alone without looking back, perhaps glad for a moment of respite from the attention my presence beside him attracts.

"You see me now, in my new clean clothes," he continues, when I catch up after one such moment of separation. He tugs on his faded gray pants. "But this is my holiday finery. I have one such suit. When I work, the clothes I wear are so patched that I think the original jacket and trousers ceased to exist a long time ago." A smile turns into a rueful laugh.

"I was declared a 'bad element' from the start. There was no changing that, I was jailed." He speaks of his travail with a heaviness of heart rather than rancor.

"Were you jailed right after liberation in 1949?"

For the moment he does not answer. Two young students with pins on their blue jackets identifying them as students from the Shanghai Foreign Languages Institute are hovering behind us with nervous smiles on their faces. These "hunters," as they are called, have heard us speaking English and are about to introduce themselves in the hopes of *parlez*-ing their way into some free language practice. Such youths are everywhere in Chinese cities, homing in on foreigners like torpedoes to practice English, now that foreigners have been semirehabilitated from their former pariah status.

Huang apparently wants nothing to do with them.

"Let's turn around," he says. The students look with surprise as we abruptly reverse rudders and head off in the opposite direction like a small convoy trying to avoid their submarine attack.

"After liberation I was put in jail right here in Shanghai," he begins again, once we have shaken the students. "They called me a counterrevolutionary. They wanted to clean my mind, I guess, although they never said why I was arrested. They just came and took me from my house and locked me up for ten years."

I suddenly recall a remark by Liu Guihai, the head judge of the Shanghai High People's Court, whom I had met the morning before. "Now we have a clear and scientific definition of the word 'counterrevolution,'" the judge had announced with both pride and satisfaction, referring to China's new legal system. "A 'counterrevolutionary act' is one that is enacted with the intent of overthrowing the government and socialist system, and endangering the People's Republic of China."

As we stop to buy a popsicle from a street-cart vendor, I ask Huang, "What do you think of the new definition of 'counterrevolutionary' and the new criminal code with its regulations limiting procedures for arrest and detention?"

For a long time, Huang concentrates on peeling off the frozen wrapper from his ice stick. Then he says firmly, "Chinese leaders are in the habit of doing what they want no matter what laws they write.

"When they took me to prison, I left my wife alone with two small children. She was ill at the time, and my babies had almost nothing to eat. They managed to stay alive only because my sister gave them a little money and succeeded in getting them some food."

Huang stares straight ahead with unfocused eyes, as if he were trying to look into the dark recesses of his own memory.

He is like a man who, awakening from a long sleep, is trying to re-establish contact with the past.

As we continue to talk, his English becomes more fluent and more animated. His recollections, at first a mere trickle, now rush forth, as if drawn into the vacuum left by the intervening years.

"Were you outwardly opposed to the revolution?" I ask.

"No. Only in my mind. But I never said anything or did anything against it. I suppose they imprisoned me because I had worked for foreigners and because some of my family members left China in 1949 for Hong Kong and the States."

"Did they put all Chinese who had worked for foreigners in jail?"

"No. But I was also a Christian. I still am." He looks up, his face registering a strange mixture of serenity and defiance. "In fact, yesterday, also for the first time in thirty years, I went to church near where I live, one of the two churches that they just reopened here in Shanghai. It was packed. There were people standing everywhere. It's the first time that I have prayed in a church for many years. I was moved to tears."

As Huang momentarily falls silent, I look up to see where we are. So engrossed have we been in our conversation that neither of us has been paying attention to where we have been going. Several times we have come to intersections and found ourselves marooned in traffic in the middle of the street because we did not scramble quickly enough to the next curb. At one spot, just before the Garden Bridge, a traffic policeman in an observation tower actually yelled at us through his PA system, "Go back. You go back!" sending us both retreating in disarray toward Huangpu Park.

But now we find ourselves walking down the Bund along the river where, at night, couples crowd up against the cement wall, arms around each other, squeezed in so tightly that it is not easy to tell where one couple begins and the next couple ends. The young people line up like birds on a telephone wire, glad for the dark privacy of the Huangpu River in front of them, oblivious of the crowds which boil up and down the sidewalk behind them—a new world of youthful courtship and romance coming alive again in China. But this seems a distant reality from all that has transpired during Huang's life.

Across Zhongshan Road stands the skyline of Shanghai, a long strip of European-style buildings built by the British, French, Japanese, and Americans, when imperialists ran the city. These buildings still dominate the Bund like old film sets, too massive to remove or replace for the next production. They evoke an era that is now hardly imaginable, when China was a European "adventurer's paradise," as the Chinese endlessly describe it.

Huang follows my gaze along the incongruous skyline of buildings, which is more suggestive of Paris or London than any Chinese city. The old Hong Kong–Shanghai Bank, now the municipal headquarters of the Shanghai Revolutionary Committee; the old Cathay Hotel—now the Peace Hotel—with its marble lobby and chic rooms with splendid views of the port and river; the Palace Hotel; the British-run Shanghai Club; the Customs House. Tonight, they are festooned with lights, red bunting, and political slogans for the holiday. Heaven knows what memories these ghost-like monuments to Shanghai's past must summon forth in Huang, whose incarceration began just as China's liberation was proclaimed, at that last moment before the West disappeared from China.

"Is it still dangerous to admit that you are a Christian?" I ask, breaking the lull in our conversation.

"I suppose it's all right," he replies distantly. "Of course, it's not nearly as bad as it once was. But for me," he adds, coming to life, "I will admit it to anyone. If they want to arrest me, I will go gladly, just like Jesus. He was a peaceable man."

"Are you ever angry at the way your country has treated you?"

"What good would that do?" he replies with a cryptic smile. "It is strange how foreigners get angry at their own countries. But we Chinese cannot change our country."

He shakes his head with resignation. "It is my country. I don't understand how all this could have come to pass in my life, how I came to be seen as the enemy. It was so long ago. I am sixty-one now. I was only thirty-one when I was imprisoned. And all I did was to take a job with foreigners because that was where opportunity lay at the time. Since then, I have been hibernating. I haven't read. I haven't written. I haven't spoken to anyone. I have hardly even thought. I had to learn how *not* to think, because it was so painful and so perilous. Thoughts could make you do dangerous things. Everything was so futile for me, and I felt so helpless. I couldn't even take care of my children." He sighs and stares down at his feet.

"For thirty years I have spoken to almost no one but my wife. If I think about it, or if I were to allow my dreams to run away freely, I think I might burst."

By now, both of us are beginning to get tired, since we have been walking for almost two hours. But there is no question of stopping, for there is hardly any place in the entire city where a foreigner can pause with a Chinese without attracting crowds of onlookers. So, once again we turn around and double back on the other side of Zhongshan Road along the Bund.

"China has a bright future," says Huang, as if he did not wish to dwell too long on the gloomy side of life. "For my two children, I have real hopes. My girl is engaged to be married. But since our family is so poor, it is hard for my son to find a wife. All the young Shanghai women now love to dress up and spend money on new clothes, getting their hair done, and having a good time. So my son's future remains a little uncertain."

"How did your children bear up having their father in prison?"

"In the beginning they suffered a great deal. What could be worse in China than for a small child to have his father in prison and have to cope with all the gossip about him being some sort of political criminal?"

We cross a street amidst a sea of people.

"Well, one day they just told me I could go home. No reason given. It was just like when they arrested me. From that day on I never spoke to anyone of my past. I did not want to remind them. I did not even look up old friends, people who had had similar experiences in prison. It was too dangerous. In truth, my wife and I have had almost no friends since I left prison."

"Did your children turn against you or criticize you during any of the political campaigns?"

Huang does not answer this question. His eyes squint and he furrows his brow. He looks down at the sidewalk. His silence is eloquent testimony to whatever agony he endured as a father whose family was driven apart by the political storms which swept back and forth across China.

"I would like to give you my address, but I don't dare," he says as we pause in front of the grand old British Consulate —now an uninviting club for visiting sailors—with characters affixed to its tile roof reading: LONG LIVE THE GREAT UNITY OF THE PEOPLES OF THE WORLD.

"If anyone saw me stop, write, and then hand you something, they might suspect me. I doubt I will see anyone I know, because this isn't my neighborhood. But you can never tell. Anyway, it would not be good if you ever came and visited me at my house. Everyone in my neighborhood would immediately want to know what I was doing with a foreigner. In the small neighborhoods here in Shanghai there is absolutely no privacy. So we could not meet there. I'm sorry."

We walk to the other side of the Garden Bridge, where the old Astor House Hotel still stands.

"You know, I have a brother in Los Angeles," he says tentatively but succinctly, as if he were not quite sure whether or not to divulge this fact.

"I wrote him for the first time eight months ago. He sent us some money, which I received, but no letter. I have written him seven times since but have received no reply back. I don't know if he is getting my letters. In any event, I cannot tell him my real situation by mail."

"Would you like me to try to contact him when I return to the United States?"

For a long while Huang says nothing. Perhaps he is trying to calculate whether all the confidences he has betrayed to me might somehow boomerang against him.

"Yes," he finally replies.

"Then I must have his address."

"Yes. Please tell him everything I have said to you. Tell him if I had a chance, I would leave China."

Without explanation, Huang begins to walk away from me across the road toward the towering Shanghai Mansions, once the Broadway Mansions, built as an apartment house by Westerners in the 1930s.

As he reaches the other side, where Caucasians are often seen, since it is now a residence for "foreign experts," he reaches into his faded gray trousers.

Almost involuntarily, I find myself following him across the street. I catch up with him just as he has passed the main entrance to the Shanghai Mansions. As I approach his side, he reaches out inconspicuously and presses a small piece of paper into my palm.

"Thank you, my friend," he says, almost whispering, without looking at me.

For a moment we walk silently beside one another as if we were two strangers. Then, without speaking, he reaches over, takes my hand, and holds it for the briefest instant in his own before sheering off my side and disappearing into the crowd.

Los Angeles

Sunday, February 4, a brilliantly clear day, stuns even the most hardened Los Angelenos, as a panorama of snow-capped mountains emerges out of the usual smog.

At eight in the morning, one hour before Disneyland usually opens, the vice-premier and minister in charge of science and technology, Fang Yi, is driven into the complex through a rear entrance.

Alighting from his black Cadillac limousine, he stands alone for a moment looking up into the dazzling morning sky as a police helicopter rattles in lazy circles overhead. It is still chilly, and Fang wears a black wool topcoat over his gray Sun Yat-sen tunic. The sleeves of what looks like a home-made brown sweater protrude from the cuffs of his jacket, suggesting an ambience totally at odds with this capital of American leisure technology.

As he lingers beside his limousine, uncertain of what is to follow, two press photographers who have been awaiting his arrival close in on him, their motor-driven cameras whirring. Watching them advance, Fang turns his head slightly to one side, as if gripped by an inner reflex to hide the large purple birthmark that surrounds his forehead and right eye. The slightness of this figure standing before me in such an unlikely setting hardly suggests his power. It is difficult to remember that this graying man is one of the key architects of China's bold new modernization program and has come to the U.S. to decide what expertise China will borrow.

No sooner has Fang signed the Disneyland guestbook than a fully uniformed band appears and begins to play shrill, leaden march music. Fang turns uneasily toward this paramilitary assemblage of musicians. For a moment, it looks as if he cannot decide whether to review them or bolt the premises. Suddenly, a flotilla of Walt Disney characters materializes. Goofy, Donald Duck, Minnie Mouse, and a donkey surround

Fang as if he were the sacrificial object in some uncatalogued pagan rite. They prance and twist in circles around him, their bulbous heads bobbing in time to the music.

Fang, frail and awkward, stands stiffly in place, uncertain how to deport himself without offending his hosts, the Disneyland officials on the sidelines who beam with satisfaction at this grand moment of cultural union.

Suddenly, Minnie jerks out of the circle and lurches up to Fang. Like a stripper in a burlesque house, she grinds her body closer and closer, raising her arms to her ever-smiling plastic face as if to seduce him into dancing.

At first, the embarrassed and confused Fang demurs. Then, at a loss, he relents and finally offers her one limp hand. She grasps it. For an excruciating few moments he takes a series of clumsy, shuffling steps with her—a captive of Disneyland—before mercifully being released.

It is painful enough that this shy sixty-four-year-old man should be coaxed into dancing in front of TV cameras like a trained bear with a plastic mouse, but it is unbearable that there are not even any children present who might add innocent delight to this otherwise macabre adult spectacle.

Providentially, the Disney offspring soon go jerking and bouncing back from whence they came. The expressionless band, which doubtless has played for kings, queens, dictators, party leaders, and presidents far more renowned than Fang Yi, departs as well, evincing no interest whatsoever in today's visitor, and Fang himself is hustled away to his next stop, a nine-screen indoor wrap-around movie theater showing a specially made film, *America the Beautiful*.

As Fang departs, I am still reeling from the impact of this scene. In these first months of Sino-American infatuation, the Chinese seem to be hurtling down the incline of westernization with little concern for braking their gathering speed. They have been ordering steel mills, fertilizer plants, hotels, jet aircraft, soft drink and cigarette factories, as if there were no tomorrow. Although they will ultimately rein in a bit, at this moment I am struck once again by the awesome attracting power of the West—a power with which the Chinese have had ample historical experience—which they now seem to ignore their passion for "modernization." Once so adamant in reminding their people and the world of the dangers of the West, China's leaders seem to have suddenly lost the power of historical analogy.

Having accompanied Fang from Washington to Los Angeles as he toured factories, technical institutes, space centers, aircraft plants, and oil-drilling-equipment corporations, I find myself unable to imagine how he and his cohorts can finally manage to knit their American adventure together with the "Chinese Revolution."

"Conditions are not the same in China as in the U.S.," Fang tells me in an interview as we fly high above Texas in a U.S. Air Force presidential jet. "We want to absorb those things from you which are good and advanced, and try our best to avoid the unsuitable aspects."

This sounds reasonable, but as I look around the sun-filled drawing room of this apotheosis of American know-how, crammed with every imaginable piece of communications technology, I cannot help but wonder how easily Fang will fit this into his view of the world.

"Do you fear that the mass importation of Western technology into China might have undesirable side effects?"

"These were fears when China was very weak," replies Fang, hardly pondering the question before answering. "That's no longer true. We are not afraid of that possibility now, just as you Americans are not afraid of us influencing you through more cultural contact.

"In introducing Western technology, we will import only those features which are useful to us, and not those which are unsuited to the conditions in our own country," he continues matter-of-factly, making my question sound overly fearful and elaborate.

In his confidence that China can separate out those things which are "useful" from those which are "unsuitable," I hear an eerie echo of China's nineteenth-century importers of Western technology. Facing a half-century of humiliating Western incursions, the "self-strengtheners," as they came to be called, were forced to deal with the reality of the West's superior technology and even to study the mechanical secrets of these adversaries, people they considered "barbarians." The problem Chinese leaders faced then as now was how to adapt Western machinery, communications systems, and armaments—which they assumed they could separate from Western values—to the reality of China.

Thus, in their initial attempts to "borrow" from the West, they devised elaborate but eventually useless formulas to help them select the best from East and West. Numerous nineteenth-century Chinese homilies endeavored to separate "practical" things, which could be imported from the West, from "essential" features, spiritual or philosophical values, which would be retained from Chinese culture. The renowned "self-strengthener" and reformer Zhang Zhidong divided everything neatly into two categories, ti (fundamental principles) and yong (practical application), so that China would have some criteria for sifting the benign from the malignant in its attempt to learn from the West.

"If we wish to make China strong and preserve Chinese learning [today, one might read "Maoist ideology"], we must promote Western learning," wrote Zhang Zhidong in 1898, as the Chinese study of technology ballooned into a confused fascination with Western philosophy and political systems as well. "But unless we first use Chinese learning to consolidate our essence and give our purpose a right direction, the strong will become rebellious and the weak will become slaves. The consequences will become worse than not being versed in Western learning at all. So, scholars should master the [Confucian] classics in order to understand the purpose of our early sagas and teachers in establishing our doctrine. . . . After this, we can select whatever Western learning can make up for our shortcomings and adopt those Western governmental methods which can cure our illness. In this way, China will derive benefit from Western learning without incurring any danger."

Without such distinctions as *ti* and *yong*, Zhang feared that China's "fundamental principles" would be corrupted by Western learning, and that her first efforts to modernize would be like "riding a horse without a bridle or sailing a ship without a rudder." Unfortunately, it turned out that even with a rudder, a Chinese ship in Western waters could easily go astray.

There was a touching nobility to Zhang's efforts to compartmentalize and tame the torrents of Western influence which were about to flood into China. In the end, though, his search for a magic filter through which Western technology could be strained to separate out the constructive from the seditious proved as futile as the medieval search for the Holy Grail.

"*Ti* and *yong* mean the same thing," wrote the brilliant translator and commentator Yan Fu in critiquing Zhang's formulations. "I have never heard that the left hand and right hand can be considered respectively as fundamental principles and application. Western knowledge has its own principles and application. If the two are separate, each can be independent; if they are combined, both will perish."

It proved much more difficult to integrate the dynamic and unruly world of Western technology into Chinese life and culture than the nineteenth-century reformers had supposed. They found that in order to make use of Western armaments and industry, Chinese had to go abroad to study and learn to read and speak foreign languages. In return, the Imperial Government had to allow foreign technicians into the heartland of China. Inexorably, foreign customs and values followed and were absorbed in spite of China's resistance.

There seemed no end to the foreign influence until, by the 1920s, China had even generated a class of urban intelligentsia preoccupied with imitating Western ways. The great Chinese essayist and short-story writer Lu Xun called these Western afficionados "imitation foreign devils." So potent had foreign influence become that during this period the word *yang*, or "foreign," attached to a product's name frequently became the hallmark of quality.

It became increasingly obvious that foreign technology and foreign culture were inseparable, and that they comprised a form of domination far subtler but every bit as powerful as imperialism itself. It was not possible to separate the two and ship "Western technology" off to China to work like an obedient team of borrowed horses. Technology was not a trained animal that would obey anyone's command and jump through hoops. It was more like a "wild beast" (as the Chinese were fond of calling foreigners in the early days), which, at any minute, might leap out of its confinement and ravage its custodians.

Whereas during Zhang and Yan's time a debate raged within the Imperial Court over the wisdom of allowing "Western learning" into China, more recently the Central Committee of the Chinese Communist party has been engaged in an analogous controversy, one in which Fang's faction has at least temporarily won the argument in favor of allowing major inseminations of foreign technology into China.

"Do you fear that the suddenness with which China has begun to court the West and introduce foreign technology might prove disruptive?" I ask Fang in our airborne interview.

"The introduction of technology is *not* a sudden thing for

China, nor is it on a large scale," he insists. "We are not importing technology regardless of our conditions, in a blind way, so to speak. We have no apprehension that because of a material improvement in the lives of our people anything will go awry."

Fang's offhand dismissal of the question surprises me, for even as we talk the impact of the Western *ti*, which travels like a virus even on the crates of a Coca-Cola bottling plant, seems to be having a profound effect on China. Only a month after Fang's departure from America to Peking, an article appeared in the *People's Daily*, belying his conviction that nothing will "go awry" as a result of his government's new policies.

"The people's thinking has become much livelier," writes an unidentified commentator in a March 1979 issue, ". . . but there are some who do not really understand what emancipated thinking means. . . . When we say we should learn from advanced foreign science and technology, they conclude that everything foreign must be good, even the bourgeois way of life.

"When we say we must not follow Marxism–Leninism–Mao-Zedong thought dramatically, they think it is no longer a guiding line.

"When we expose the difficulties and problems caused by Lin Biao and the Gang of Four and by our own shortcomings and mistakes, they doubt the superiority of the socialist system."

I ask Fang, "Does the Chinese leadership have any systematic formulation of what they hope Chinese society will look like after modernization?"

"That would be very hard to say," he replies. "I cannot answer that myself. I cannot speculate on what it will be like after the year 2000 because it is so far away."

Pressing him on his vague response, I tell him how surprised I am that in a society as planned as China's, there is not a more coherent plan. "How can China develop into a rational society without a clearer conception of where it wishes to go?" I ask.

"We have a State Planning Commission that has worked out long-term as well as immediate plans," he says, indicating that he has little interest in pursuing the subject.

"Do you think that the reintroduction of foreign technicians, businessmen, and teachers could ever again presage the kinds of resentful anti-foreign outbreaks which have been numerous throughout Chinese history?" I ask.

"There is no danger of that!" Fang dismisses the idea as if it were not only dangerous but unthinkable. "These anti-foreign trends were only a phenomenon during the latter part of the Qing dynasty [around the time of the Boxer Rebellion, at the end of China's last imperial dynasty]. That was a feudal society, whereas ours is now a socialist society."

Reminded of anti-foreign incidents as recently as the Cultural Revolution, Fang quickly adds, "During the Cultural Revolution, the Gang of Four and Lin Biao did show some of these tendencies—for instance, when we wanted to introduce some advanced technologies from the West—but they criticized this as a slavish philosophy of worshipping foreign things. However, this was an erroneous view. Science and technology are things which countries can exchange."

"How do you resolve the obvious contradiction between Mao's policy of self-reliance on the one hand and China's new willingness to rely on both foreign technology and capital on the other?"

"In the main, our policy is one of relying on our own efforts but also of seeking foreign assistance if possible. We are internationalists. Chairman Mao taught us that there should be no contradiction between self-reliance and learning from others."

Indeed, Mao made many statements, particularly during those periods of his life when he was more favorably disposed toward the West, suggesting that China did need to learn from abroad.

"To advocate wholesale westernization is wrong. China has suffered a great deal from the mechanical absorption of foreign material," Mao wrote in 1940. "But, to nourish our own culture, China needs to assimilate a good deal of progressive foreign culture, not enough of which was done in the past. . . . However, we should not gulp any of this foreign material down uncritically, but must treat it as we do our food—first chewing it, then submitting it to the working of the stomach and the intestines with their juices and secretions, and separating it into nutriment to be absorbed, and the waste matter discarded before it can nourish us."

Looking for textual support, Fang Yi would doubtless agree with this vintage Mao and ignore statements from other times when Mao and the Chinese leadership evinced a less tolerant attitude toward learning from abroad, times when he viewed it as a dangerous and unnecessary crutch which, in the long run, would hurt China more than help it.

Momentarily, my airborne conversation with Fang Yi is interrupted. Two smartly uniformed U.S. Air Force stewards appear to offer Fang a choice of soft drinks. He chooses a Fresca. "It is not possible for any country to isolate itself from the world," he continues as he sips his drink from a plastic glass.

"What has happened to all those Chinese who, until recently, so strenuously opposed foreign borrowing and even technological specialization?" I ask.

"They were subject to criticism by our people. But we view each case on its own merits. Just like when some reporter asked Vice-Premier Deng what had happened to former Foreign Minister Qiao Guanhua, and he said, 'Qiao is still eating his meals and sleeping every night. But he committed grave errors.'"

"Are you so sure that the process of modernization will go as smoothly as you seem to indicate?"

"Of course, in actual practice, it is quite possible that mistakes of one kind or another may occur," he answers matter-of-factly.

"For many Americans agreements such as those between China and the R.J. Reynolds tobacco company, and the Coca-Cola Company have come to symbolize the hazards of too rapid westernization. How do such agreements fit into China's vision of her future?"

"This is a simple matter," replies Fang, as if he were going to unlock the riddle of the universe in a single sentence. "We want to have foreign visitors in very great numbers. These foreign visitors, tourists, want to drink Coca-Cola. They are accustomed to it. As for us Chinese, we prefer our green tea."

By now our plane is beginning its descent over the Sierra Nevada Mountains, en route to the private runway of the Lockheed Corporation in Palmdale, California.

As I leave Fang's stateroom, I am still wondering whether this generation of Chinese will be any more successful than its predecessors in separating off the *yong*, or practical aspects, of American technology from the companies and culture which will export them. Fang's single-minded determination to see his country modernize is indeed impressive. But I am perplexed by the way that he and others evade any discussion of the possible consequences of their policies, the way they have so facilely "reversed the verdict" on Mao's ideology of self-reliance, suggesting that apparent contradictions are actually only in the mind of the beholder.

Confronting China since Deng's rise to power is a little like meeting an old friend who has been so totally transformed by a new religion or cult that you begin to doubt you ever really knew him.

Confronting Fang Yi makes me wonder how this advocate of

Western technology has laid to rest the old slogans of "class struggle," "anti-imperialism," and "putting politics in command." Does he now feel any lingering affinity for these discarded political concepts? What was he thinking during those bleak years of the cultural revolution and the Gang of Four, and how did he survive?

As Fang steps off the U.S. presidential jet at the Lockheed plant and is greeted by Governor Jerry Brown, my mind drifts back to the time I spent in China while Mao was alive and his "thought" still held sway. As I watch Fang disappear into a massive hangar, surrounded by solicitous Lockheed executives in corporate dress, all hoping for lucrative aircraft contracts with China, one of the points that Mao and the Gang of Four harped on relentlessly snaps into clearer focus. Whatever the impractical and oppressive aspects of Mao's isolationism, he did unsparingly stress the need for China to be independent and self-reliant. He tirelessly expressed his belief that new technology would have to develop on home soil if it were ever to take root successfully in China. If there was anything which China's experience with the West had brought home with clarity, claimed Mao, it was that there was nothing neutral about technology; that it could not be simply divorced from the culture that creates and exploits it; that it could not be exported, sanitized of all traces of the world in which it was developed: there is no *yong* separate from its *ti*.

Should veterans of Western borrowing like Zhang Zhidong and Yan Fu now be reading the *People's Daily* in their ultimate repose, they might well be smiling quaintly at the notion that this generation of Chinese could succeed in harnessing the West to China's purposes where they had failed. In their time, they watched the fall of China's last dynasty, the dissolution of Confucian culture, and the fracturing of China's identity. Now, with China's modern Marxist emperor, Mao Zedong, gone from his residence at Zhongnanhai within the walls of the old Imperial City, and so much of what he stood for being erased, it is perhaps time to cast a historical look backward. As China again sets her sights westward, one wonders if the prophecy of the Imperial Grand Secretary Wo Ren might be fulfilled. He warned the Qing dynasty court in 1867 that "after several years, Western learning will end in nothing less than driving the multitude of Chinese people into allegiance with the barbarians."

Dairen

Kunming Street, in the Manchurian seaport city of Dairen, has been blockaded from traffic. The several blocks which rise on a slight grade up from Zhungshan Street and the train station are choked with peasants who squat along the curbside selling their wares just as they might have in an old-time bazaar. Indeed, walking in their midst is like being in a time warp, for it was precisely this kind of unruly, self-motivated merchant that the Chinese Revolution once seemed intent upon eradicating. So strenuous were official efforts to banish this sort of commerce from the streets that most Chinese cities were completely emptied of sidewalk peddlers.

But now, Manchuria's peasantry has quietly stolen back to the streets to hawk produce, seafood, and dry goods, pocketing the proceeds as if Chairman Mao, the Great Leap Forward, the Cultural Revolution, and the Gang of Four had never existed. Kunming Street is a veritable free-fire zone for private enterprise.

"Yes. Yes. I think it's quite wonderful," says Wang Weijing, a thoughtful and earnest young instructor from the Dairen Institute of Railways who has been shopping here at the Dairen Free Market and become my self-appointed guide for the morning. "It has grown a great deal since it opened last March. At first there were just a few brave people. Then the word got around that it was actually all right to come and sell things privately here. And now look at it!" He gestures paternally out across the crowd.

The market extends for several blocks. People sit almost shoulder to shoulder on both curbs selling their wares. Consumers push and jostle each other, trying to work their way up the street, shopping bags filled with seafood, vegetables, and fruit. They are joined by a large number of people who do not appear to be at the Free Market to buy anything at all but have come rather as a form of entertainment. They cluster around a customer who is bargaining with a fishmonger, enjoying the miniature drama. They listen with absorption to an aggressive merchant making pitches for the healing powers of his herbal medicine or the efficacy of his brushes and pot scrubbers.

"They used to say that in order to be truly revolutionary you had to be poor," says Wang, walking beside me and delivering an explanatory monologue like a museum guide. "So, no one dared do anything. They wouldn't let the peasants have their own private plots. If they caught you selling goods like this, they would reprimand you. They really made a mess out of things."

Wang is in his mid-twenties, and despite his apparent enthusiasm for this new post–Gang of Four peasant capitalism, he is also one of the thirty-five million Chinese who are members of the Chinese Communist party. He wears nondescript black shoes and a gray jacket over a blue sweatshirt-like garment that doubles as underwear here in North China. His hair is short with a whirlpool cowlick in the back. Of modest build and pale complexion, he radiates thoughtfulness and friendliness.

"The economy suffered a lot here during the Cultural Revolution," he says as we stop before a bounteous heap of Chinese cabbage that has been unceremoniously dumped on the sidewalk. Three women rummage through the pile looking for an acceptable head.

"Many people suffered. It was impossible to do any serious work or to learn anything," Wang is saying. "Everything was closed down: schools, factories, government offices, state farms. No one worked! It was a frightening thing to see a whole country stop work. It was chaos!"

He brightens. "Now, we are seeking stability. The Gang of Four used to say, 'The world is in great disorder. What an excellent situation!' But how can you run a country when every day there are drastic changes, no consistent policy at all? If government policy reverses itself every few years, no one will know what to do."

As one so often hears in China, Wang's critique of changes in political lines embraces every change but the last one. Like all Chinese who struggle to maintain a belief that the present policy, the latest permutation of "lines," is the right one, Wang cannot quite allow himself to imagine that today's politics, even the Free Market, may yet prove to be tomorrow's erroneous line.

"Now, the government allows people much more flexibility," he continues with enthusiasm. "Yes. People *can* make more money. But look! Now they *want* to produce." He pauses, and almost affectionately surveys the scene around us.

It is a beehive of activity, an outdoor supermarket capable of providing for almost every daily need. Although it has no aisles, it does have a rough supermarketlike organization so that vendors selling similar goods are positioned together. However, since many people actually sell the same wares sitting side by side, it is infinitely more competitive than a supermarket. It reminds one more of Miracle Mile on Auto Row, where all the car dealers gravitate together, not because they enjoy the competition but because they know that by centralizing themselves, they will attract more customers.

At the beginning of Kunming Street, the shoemakers have set up shop, spreading their scraps of leather, buckles, and rubber soles around their portable stitching machines. A little farther up the street, several elderly men, with their displays spread out on small dropcloths beside tattered charts of the human body, sell potions and herbal remedies. Beside them sit vendors selling household goods, such as pots, knives, and choppers as well as a few articles of clothing, including plastic sandals, belts, and handkerchiefs.

As Wang and I walk on, we run into the largest and most active section of the market, where old peasants are selling seafood.

"You see very few young people here," explains Wang. "Most of them have jobs in factories. The Free Market is mostly for older people who cannot do such strenuous labor any more. They pay a few cents to the city for a license, and then they're able to come and make a little money to help out their families."

The peasants sit on the curbs chatting and selling. Some of the men smoke long-stemmed pipes. They sit in front of piles of bubbling green crabs whose claws are tied with straw thongs so they will not nip customers or escape, and open burlap bags filled with cockles, clams, oysters, fish, and shrimp. Across the street are heaps of squid, eels, sea slugs, jellyfish, octopus, and other even less familiar creatures of the deep.

Housewives with plastic net shopping bags surge in around the peddlers, inspecting, touching, smelling, and feeling the goods before they buy.

"I think that things will continue on in a stable fashion for a long time," says Wang hopefully, "because the people support the leadership. They have more power now. They are able to vote for their own local committees and delegates. We have a new criminal code and constitution which will prevent opportunists from recklessly climbing over everyone again to the top."

I am sure Wang believes what he says, and perhaps his prophecies will indeed come to pass. Nonetheless, as I listen to him talk, I cannot erase memories of all those seemingly enthusiastic Chinese during the Gang of Four period who were equally eager to justify all that their government was then doing. Like Wang, they too were polemical in tone, their explanations aimed as much at banishing their own doubts as convincing visitors of the correctness of their government's policies.

Like so many other educated Chinese for whom respite has at last arrived after a long and bleak voyage, Wang evinces a desire to erase and forget the past, as if one could start from ground zero by a simple flick of a switch. These defenders of China's current policies and its dalliance with the West focus only on the present and the future, cataloguing the curing powers of factory bonuses and free markets as if there were no yesterday. They speak of the past as if it were a closed case that demanded no explanation beyond the incantation of certain leaders' names at whose feet the whole debacle can be laid. They are relieved to bury the past, even if in a shallow grave, without giving any believable explanation for its successes or failures. They show an almost universal tendency to shy away from rehashing the pain and confusion through which they have just lived, as if mere discussion might somehow cause that past to be reborn.

Unaware of my thoughts, Wang says optimistically, "I think that our future will be bright. The government is now paying the peasants twenty percent more for their grain, so of course they are happier. Who wouldn't like to make more money?"

Evidence of his argument visibly abounds. The Free Market is not only crowded but also open seven days a week, including holidays, from sunup to sunset.

"Of course, we charge a little more on holidays," says a grizzled old man sitting in front of a sack of dried shrimp.

"I can get more for these sea slugs and crabs in the morning than in the evening because they're fresher," adds a woman who has brought in two kinds of seafood from the country on the train. "We can't take these things home at night and bring them back the next day." She laughs. "They would go bad! But that's the way with the Free Market."

"People often assume that the plight of the peasant is much worse than that of a city worker," says Wang as we walk on. "They think that the peasants don't get as much meat to eat, or that life is hard because they live in more primitive houses. But, you know, actually many peasants are richer than city workers, because in the countryside their expenses are less. Often you can't buy a house in the city even if you have the money. People have to live all cooped up in small apartments. But out in the countryside, you can build a nice house yourself on land that your work brigade will give you. You can raise a lot of your own food, and you don't spend a lot of money on things like busses and movies."

"Won't all this private initiative end up with some people becoming wealthy while others stay poor, exactly the kind of inegalitarian society that Chairman Mao warned against?"

"No," he replies emphatically. "The real intention of Chairman Mao was to make people rich. But he wanted the *majority*, not the minority, to become rich. In the past, most people suffered at the hands of a few."

We pause before an old peasant who is selling a variety of minuscule shellfish that looks something like a snail. When Wang and I stop to look, he stands and offers one of his tiny gastropods to us for inspection.

"They're very tasty," he says, smiling shyly through a set of decayed teeth.

"How do you get them out so you can eat them?" I ask, examining the narrow orifice into the shell.

"Oh. You cook them in boiling water and then suck them out."

"Do people like this Free Market?"

"Yes, indeed. Yes." He waves his hand over his head. "Pretty soon it will be too big for Kunming Street." As if he has suddenly decided I was some kind of inspecting official to whom appeals could be addressed, he adds, "They ought to build a regular market with real booths and a place to get in out of the rain and cold in the winter."

"Are you worried about people in China becoming too concerned with materialism?" I ask Wang as the old man turns to a customer.

He feigns surprise. "Why? If I could get a car, I would think that was wonderful." His face grows radiant at the thought. "When I was a small child, I never dreamed of owning such a thing as a car, or even a TV. Although those things may seem very commonplace to you in America, they were unimaginable to us.

"No! No! Don't worry about the Chinese people becoming materialistic! That's exactly what the Chinese people need: more things and better food to improve their lives. Why should we be satisfied with so little when others have so much?"

"What do you think of all the billboards that are springing up on the streets and the advertisements in the newspapers and on television? Could that sort of thing lead to a restoration of capitalism?"

"No. I love to see them," replies Wang with relish. "I wish they would print even more advertisements in the newspapers telling people what was available in the stores and what they cost. That way there would be a bigger turnover. Isn't the object of socialism to get the necessary goods for life into the hands of the people who need them?"

Just up the street from the Free Market's seafood section are the fruits and vegetables. Since it is fall, there is an abundance of apples, pears, squash, and cabbage.

Wang and I stop in front of an old woman who, besides selling eggs, has three scrofulous chickens for sale. Still alive, they are tethered by strings tied from their feet to her ankle.

"Four yuan for this one," she announces assertively, picking up the fattest chicken by the neck. It looks at us with wide, unknowing eyes.

"Or this one for three yuan," she continues, letting the first bird fall back to the pavement with a thump and a squawk, while grabbing for a lusterless bird with almost no feathers.

"No, thank you."

"How about some eggs, then?" she asks, putting down the second chicken and picking up two eggs, one in each hand.

"We're just looking," Wang says to her. As we walk away from the egg seller I ask Wang, "What would happen now in China if a wealthy person died? Could he leave his savings and house to his children?"

"Yes, of course," replies Wang, as if this would be the most obvious thing imaginable. "That is also legal."

"Would he be taxed?"

"No. For instance, I have a friend whose father just left him a lot of money. He's got it now in a savings account, and they've just raised the interest rate, too. And no one taxed him or even said anything about it to him. But you should remember that in a country like China, most people hardly have anything to leave when they die. We are still not a rich country. Here, if someone finally can afford to buy a watch, they are very happy. I don't think that is true in your country."

"Won't such inheritance laws tend to create a class of people who become wealthy without working?"

"No. At least not now. I mean, if my father works hard and passes his money on to me, and I become rich, that's fine. If I don't have to work, that's fine, too. Who could blame anyone who was wealthy for not working? There aren't enough jobs now anyway."

Then, feeling that he might have gone a little bit too far in extolling the limitless possibilities for the jobless accumulation of wealth under the new regime, Wang quickly adds, "But most people do not want to retire and be idle."

"And what happens if a Chinese citizen has a relative

abroad who sends him a great deal of money? Is there any limitation?"

"Why? The person is free to spend the money as he sees fit."

"Do you think that will help create a classless society?"

"Maybe not, but it's legal."

"Do you think legality is replacing equality as the new yardstick of what is right and wrong?"

Wang smiles, but does not answer.

"China used to boast that it was a country free of unemployment and inflation," I say, trying a different track. "Is that still true?"

"To be frank, there is unemployment," he replies as we pass a cart loaded with apples and a team of scrawny horses tied to a tree. "We have a problem now. There are too many young people graduating from middle school, and too many 'educated youth' who were sent to the countryside under the Gang of Four coming back to the cities looking for jobs. Sometimes the government assigns them to factories just to get them a salary. But the factories don't want them. So, it's a problem. There are too many Chinese people. Now the government is trying to carry out a comprehensive birth-control program. They are giving people incentives for having only one child. You know, give them priorities in housing, better schools."

"But how can all these unemployed youths ever expect to join this new socialist process of getting rich?"

"Well, they'll just have to wait. Just like in your country." Wang laughs, pleased at his resourceful reply to my obviously barbed question. "And then, of course, many young people are beginning to set up small businesses or co-ops on their own."

"Is that legal?"

"Yes, of course, just as the Free Market is legal. Several people can get together, pool their resources, and open a small restaurant, factory, or other business. All they need is a license."

"Could several doctors get together and set up a private office?"

"Oh, no. Impossible!" Wang is amused at the very thought. "Not trained professionals. We have a shortage of them. But people could set up a vegetable shop, a stationery store, or a bicycle-repair shop. That sort of thing is fine."

"Who decides what kind of private business is permissible?"

"Oh, well . . . there are government officials. Perhaps the people who give the licenses."

"And what would happen if a business becomes very successful?"

"If there is a profit from a co-op, it would have to be divided equally among the people who are members, according to how much they invested and how hard they worked. There is a limit though to how big something like that can get, because you can't hire labor. That would be exploitation."

"If you allow people to work on their own so that they become richer and richer and accumulate more and more money and things, how is that different from capitalism?"

"No. That's not capitalism at all. That's just what the Gang of Four said. The reason why it's not capitalism is that in a socialist society like China's, you are still not allowed to exploit people for your own profit. You cannot hire another man to work for you and make money for you. But if you work harder yourself and make more money, that's completely all right."

We are now surrounded by curious people as we hold our question-and-answer session in the middle of the street. Seeing that Wang is looking a trifle uneasy about being center stage, I suggest that we keep walking as we talk.

"Well, let's say a man worked hard in his co-op or factory,

put in a lot of overtime, sent his wife down here to the Free Market to sell handicrafts or something, and finally ended up with a good deal of savings. Could he buy an extra house and rent it out for profit?"

"Yes, I think so. The new constitution says that he has that right," Wang answers, appearing to be a little uncertain about the territory into which our conversation is now heading.

"What if he wanted to buy three or four extra houses to rent out? Would that be all right?" I press on.

"Yes. I think he could."

"How would that be any different from the old-time evil landlords?"

"Well, of course, he would not be able to charge an unreasonable rent."

"But who would determine what was a reasonable rent? And maybe with such a severe housing shortage people would be willing to slip him a little extra on the side just to get a house at all, even if it was expensive."

"Well . . . ," he begins shaking his head and laughing, "these things are very complicated. I don't really know the answers. Perhaps they haven't been worked out yet."

And perhaps it is not surprising that such details have not been worked out yet in China, if in fact there is any country where they have been.

Nonetheless, it comes as a shock to hear a Party member like Wang admit that he does not know the answer to a question, or where China is actually headed, or even that he does know China is painfully behind most Western nations.

Somehow, in the past, when China's revolutionary pretensions were more outspoken, and when it was heresy to do anything other than acquiesce to the myth of China's socialist perfection, it was easier for a visitor to overlook the vastness of the chasm which lay between fact and rhetoric. Since the Chinese were loath to acknowledge the fallibility of their vision or the weaknesses of their own country, it behooved "foreign guests" (who did not wish to appear ungrateful for being granted permission to visit) to avoid questions which might appear hostile.

But now, as the totalist rhetoric of the past fades like mist, and as the Chinese themselves admit to boggling contradictions and tirelessly point out their own "backwardness," it can be almost frightening to look beneath the surface and realize that there is no infallible grand plan, that there are only ideas and pieces which may never fit together with the symmetry and neatness that we had come to expect of the "Chinese Revolution."

Everywhere around me in China now I see irreconcilable forces and contradictions—East and West, capitalism and communism, imperialism and socialism—which no one any longer tries to hide or tame with idealistic rhetoric or organizational bullying. Indeed, such candor comes as a relief. But with all that said, it is impossible to stand in this Free Market and not wonder if all this profit-making energy will not finally collide with the collectivist ethic, which theoretically animates China.

"The truth is," adds Wang, as if now reading my thoughts, "they are still working on some of these problems." He shrugs.

His admission is a welcome relief, even though he clings to the minor fiction that somewhere there are patriotic cadres "working on" these problems, like elves toiling toward Christmas in Santa's workshop.

It feels as if the Chinese have finally become exhausted holding the pose of socialist purity and promise. For it was a pose so out of synch with the reality most Chinese were living that it sapped almost all of their energy just to maintain it. For many Chinese—at least in the cities—it seems to come as a relief to finally surrender, and at least for now, let the devil take the hindmost.

It is not difficult to rejoice in China's new attitudes, and at the same time feel a sense of loss. For although the tenacious grip with which Chinese officials used to hold to their old vision of a classless society may have been unrealistic, it also filled our time with a frightening but exhilarating sense of possibility.

By now, Wang and I have come to the end of the Free Market and turned off Kunming Street. We walk back through the central square toward the Dairen Railroad Station. Although the square is not technically a part of the Free Market, even here there are occasional carts of fruit, or individuals with a few trinkets and wares such as lamps or dishes spread out on the sidewalk for sale.

"Well," says Wang Weijing as we stop to say good-bye, "I hope I shall have a chance to come to your country someday to study. There are many things which China can learn from a developed country such as yours."

Epilogue

The last several decades of Chinese history are littered with the half-buried remains of abandoned political lines and disgraced leaders. The "correct line" of one era has become the "wrong line" of the next with such regularity that it is a wonder such a system of inevitable political obsolescence can still attract adherents. Yet, after each debacle, the Chinese rise from the ashes, ready to launch a new campaign as if the past had been surgically severed from the present.

One can only stand in awe, wondering how a people once so involved in using their history as a guide can now seem so disconnected from it; how they can start anew without either truly taking stock or losing nerve over the series of self-confessed failures which lie behind them.

In pondering the changes in China, I am reminded of the numerous marriages of certain Hollywood stars, who rapturously announce new betrothals every few years, apparently undiscouraged by the debris of ex-spouses by the wayside. I read their wedding announcements, look at their happy, smiling faces in the paper, and wonder how it is that their past reversals never undermine their ability to believe that this time it will all be different.

Perhaps, though, the capacity to consign failure to oblivion is China's greatest ally. As China's renowned essayist Lu Xun wrote in 1925: "People with good memories are liable to be crushed by the weight of suffering. Only those with bad memories, the fittest to survive, can still live on."

Abandoning memory to wipe the slate clean has its virtues, I suppose. It does clear the decks for a new start, not unlike a commercial enterprise undertaking bankruptcy procedures. But it seems to me that if a company, a country, or a political ideology wishes to remain credible, capable of evoking belief in its followers, it must not be too careless about how often it changes its mind.

Like the Red Guards who campaigned during the Cultural Revolution to have red lights signify "go," and green lights signify "stop," China's present leaders seem unperturbed by the discontinuity between their new policies and the past. But their defiance of doctrinal consistency is such that finally all their values and political judgments now have only temporary relevance.

Although as a foreigner I sometimes bridled at being relegated in pre–Gang of Four China to the category of disruptive outlander, I nonetheless had grown accustomed to my plight. In fact, as this book has suggested, I often felt that there was a certain logic to Chinese wariness of foreigners (given the history of China and the West). Now suddenly, with very little self-improvement on our own part, we foreigners find ourselves "rehabilitated" along with the thousands of Chinese who had fallen out of grace. Americans have been transformed from the status of nonpeople to be avoided to fraternal friends. Like the single kiss that transfigured the fairy-tale frog into a prince, the demise of Mao and the Gang of Four has now transformed us foreigners not only from foe to friend, but from a model to be totally eschewed into one to be emulated.

So many things have happened and so much has changed since I first visited China in early 1975, a time when almost every erg of Chinese energy still seemed focused on erasing bourgeois and foreign influences. I recall walking in the Summer Palace outside of Peking one lovely spring day of that year. Suddenly, an elderly Chinese woman, steaming through the dense crowd with her head down, unceremoniously rammed into me. Before she could even regain her balance, a guide from the China People's Association for Friendship with Foreign Countries barked harshly at her, "Watch out for the foreign guests!" The woman looked up, first at his severe countenance, then at my Caucasian face, and without uttering a word, fled fearfully back into the crowd.

To this day, I am not exactly certain why the incident remains so vividly etched in my memory. It was, of course, distressing to have my Chinese protector speak so disagreeably on my account to a hapless old woman who clearly bore me no malice. But more disturbing, he seemed to berate this unguided human missile not so much because he was worried she might hurt or disturb me (if recollection serves, she was small and had bound feet), but because he did not want to be party to any unplanned incident where Chinese and foreigners might meet, even if by quite literally bumping into each other. China's awesome powers of vigilance were focused on preventing the "foreign guests" from becoming involved in any disturbance that might ripple out into "the masses" with unplanned consequences.

Six years later, with the guard changed in the Central Committee, collisions with the West seem the order of the day. Far from avoiding contact in the streets, Chinese now contrive ways to bump into "foreign guests." This does not mean that all barriers between Chinese and Westerners are gone. Even in this heyday of Sino-American friendship many Chinese, particularly peasants and less well-educated urban workers, are still wary of unregulated contact with outsiders, while officials, having acquired a knee-jerk suspiciousness of foreigners, still show reserve. But China's intelligentsia and urban youth, far from exhibiting hesitation, now evidence a passion for Western styles and contact. As they rush toward the West, they leave behind a government of leaders that seems uncertain how to manage the ballooning exchange they themselves have initiated.

One wonders if Deng Xiaoping and Hua Guofeng, like their Qing dynasty precursors, still dream of finding the perfect formula for "barbarian management." Do they still fancy that somewhere in the welter of coming and going between China and the West they will discover the mythological filter that will strain out "function" from "essence"?

China's leaders may become periodically alarmed at the cauldron they see boiling beneath them. They may withdraw the right of their people to display wall posters. They may announce new regulations circumscribing rights of protest. They may suggest that it does not behoove prudent Chinese to follow foreigners back to their hotel rooms or visit their apartments too regularly. They may even make arrests, as they did several months after I left Peking, when the Security Bureau swept down on the Peace Café, closing it and arresting Benefit-the-People Wang, New Nation Li, and their cohorts. But by allowing continued contact with the outside world, they have started currents flowing which will not be easily reversed. As long as these currents are recharged by foreign visitors to China and Chinese going abroad, they will continue to course beneath the governmentally manipulated surface of Chinese society. Short of returning China to isolation, these currents will not abate.

In the past, it was virtually impossible to coax a letter out of China. Now it is a rare week that letters from China do not arrive in my mailbox.

"When we spent time together in public places around Peking, I felt very happy," writes Ling Mulan from Peking, in an English scattered with Chinese phrases. "It was not because I am so fearless, but only that I knew that in fact I was doing nothing wrong. Is it not natural to want to exchange ideas, opinions, tastes, etc., with a person who is from another world? Of course, as a result of the Cultural Revolution and old social conventions, people here in China do still tend to gossip about such things, particularly if they should see a Chinese girl together with a foreign man. These people are just narrow-minded, although I do not think you can call it their fault. It is a carry-over from the Gang of Four era. They don't realize that the whole world is changing. They don't understand that they should allow themselves and their minds to change with it.

"There are of course people who would give me unasked-for advice if they knew I had made friends with a foreigner like you. They might say, 'Be careful, you haven't had much experience,' or 'Make sure that you don't get yourself in trouble.' Well, perhaps some of this kind of advice is still good to hear."

In another letter, Mulan continues: "Each night in Peking there are dance parties everywhere. And by the way, I enjoy dancing very much, and hope that one day I will be able to dance in America with you. So everyhing seems to be going quite well. Recently two of my classmates went to the USA to see their relatives, and then stayed to go to university there. At first, all of us students were very surprised by this, by the fact that my friends just made an application to our government, and within two months had been given permission to be on their way. It was something I couldn't have imagined a few years ago."

Several weeks later I receive another letter from Ling Mulan. This bright and determined woman suddenly announces, "I want to tell you that in spite of any hardship and difficulties, I have made up my mind to go to college in the USA." Her decision seems at once extraordinary and predictable. For as we talked in Peking, it became obvious that the West was for her an ineluctable frontier drawing her outward.

"This decision will perhaps be the most important of my life. You may be surprised. You may think, 'How ridiculous!' But please listen to my ideas and plans with patience to see whether they are impractical."

Of course, her ideas are impractical. With little knowledge, no scholarship, and no contact besides myself, she has decided she must study in America. How will she get an exit visa? How will she pay for her airfare here, not to mention her tuition? There are endless questions which make the idea seem ludicrous. Yet, reading her letter, I am convinced that somehow she will make it.

"The present situation now favors my plan," she continues, blithely mapping her strategy like a general. "Our government has started to encourage and give permission to those who are able to go abroad for university study at their own expense. I don't know how long this policy will last. Maybe it will soon change. So, I'm afraid that the chance will pass away quickly.

"Now, the only thing—the most important thing is that I need YOUR HELP. I know it may not be proper and delicate to ask for your help in such a straight way. But please give me your understanding. I have no other choice, since opportunity knocks only once. If I lose my dream this time, perhaps I will lose all."

There is something about the force of Ling Mulan's determination that is breathtaking. She is so clear about what she needs, and so determined to attain it, that it has been a joy to help. I can understand her passion to leave China, and can completely sympathize with her as an individual. Yet, as I have begun rounding up applications for her and making other inquiries, I have also felt a little uneasy, as if I were becoming some small part of the process of draining China westward.

Huang Baoren, the man with whom I had spent the day in Shanghai, has also written a number of letters to me. Their indirection in no way disguises his desperation to hear from his brother in L.A., his only contact, besides myself, with a Western world to which he yearns to come.

"My friend," he writes in English, "have you already succeeded in contacting my brother? We are so anxious to hear of him and urgently wait his reply. I am always thinking of our meeting. Often now I go down to the end of the bridge by the Post Office to the place where we met. I stand there alone and remember our meeting as clearly as if it happened yesterday. God bless you and your whole family."

Since returning to the U.S., I have in fact tried to find a

phone listing for his brother and written numerous letters to his address. Although none were ever returned, neither were they answered.

"Perhaps we'd better stop searching for him," replies Huang after I write of my failure and offer to go to Los Angeles myself to try to find him. I know how much Huang is counting on his brother to help him leave Shanghai. "I have already waited thirty years. I may as well wait a few more. My brother must be afraid to correspond with me while I am in a 'bad situation.' Maybe he does not have enough money to help me. So, I think we'd better stop."

There is a wistful resignation in that final hand-written note which comes in an envelope so well sealed up with paste that it would have confounded even the most determined Chinese postal censor.

Not far from Huang Boaren's house, Shen Yongzhang, one of the young cyclists from Shanghai, is also busy writing letters—of quite a different kind. He sends several colored posters rolled around a piece of bamboo. There are two of Chinese opera stars, one of a pretty young Chinese woman, and one inexplicably showing a blond, tow-headed young girl who looks Scandinavian. The package is addressed in both Chinese and English. The English looks as if it has been traced off the slip of paper on which I wrote my address that night in People's Square.

"Can you tell us what young Americans are wearing now?" he asks. "Do you have any pictures? We hope that you will come back soon, because since you have left, we have not been able to meet any more foreigners."

After a few more felicitations, the next letter gets right to the point. "Have you seen the TV series *Man from Atlantis*? It is from America and is now being shown on Chinese TV. We think it is very good and wonder if it was popular in your country." Indeed, I have neither seen nor heard of *Man from Atlantis*, a reportedly forgettable science fiction series that the Chinese purchased inexpensively after they could not get *Roots*.

"Could you please send me an American picture calendar?" adds Shen in a P.S. Such a simple thing to get here, something people give away free at Christmas. But to Shen, as he turns reverently toward America, it must surely appear as an almost religious object.

Shen's vulnerability to the attracting powers of the West seems complete. Are people telling him, "Watch out for the foreign guests"? And if they are, can he understand what they are saying, or perhaps should be saying? Or does he view them only as hounding cadres who cannot see the exciting flow of Western people, ideas, and commodities just beyond the ends of their political noses?

Whether or not China will again be pulled drastically out of its own orbit by its new proximity to the powerful gravitational field of America is still not clear. But something that Ling Mulan said back in Peking months before she herself decided that her destiny lay in the U.S. still echoes in my mind.

"We Chinese have traditionally been cut off from outside influences. I think we often resist foreign ideas at first. But when foreign influences finally do make an impact, we don't seem to know where to stop. We don't seem to know how to balance. Suddenly some people want to get rid of everything Chinese and have everything foreign."

Orville Schell, born in New York in 1940, was graduated from Harvard University and then spent several years in the Far East studying Chinese. He covered the war in Indochina, then returned to do Ph.D. work at the University of California at Berkeley. He has been back to China three times in the past four years.

Mr. Schell has written for *The New Yorker, Life, Rolling Stone, Look, Atlantic Monthly*, and many other publications. He is the author of *In The People's Republic*, co-editor of the first three volumes of *The China Reader*, and co-author of *Modern China*. His other books include *The Town That Fought To Save Itself* and *Brown*.

DATE DUE

NO 2'81			
NO 16'81			
GAYLORD			PRINTED IN U.S.A.